ISSUES MANAGEMENT

**How You Can Plan, Organize and
Manage For the Future**

Joseph F. Coates
Vary T. Coates
Jennifer Jarratt
Lisa Heinz

This book is based on a research report prepared by **J. F. Coates, Inc.** for the **Electric Power Research Institute (EPRI).**

LOMOND
1986

Library of Congress Catalog Number: 86-081280

ISBN: 0-912338-55-5 (Clothbound)
ISBN: 0-912338-56-3 (Microfiche)

Chapters 2-4 of this book comprise a report submitted by J.F. Coates, Inc. to the Electric Power Research Institute (EPRI) and published by EPRI under the title, *Issues Identification and Management: The State of The Art of Methods and Techniques* (P-4143, July 1985). Chapter 5 is drawn from another report by J.F. Coates, Inc. to EPRI, *Issues Identification and Management: Developing a Research Agenda* (P-4488, March 1986). EPRI holds the copyright to that material and has kindly granted limited permission to Lomond Publications, Inc. to reproduce it in this book.

Lomond Publications, Inc.
P.O. Box 88
Mt. Airy, MD 21771

TABLE OF CONTENTS

Publisher's Note vii
Preface ix
Acknowledgements xi

1 LOOKING TO THE FUTURE 1

    Our World Has Changed 1
    Technological Blunders 5
    Greater Risks 5
    The Availability of Institutional and Personnel
       Resources for Future Studies 6
    Serious Futurism 7
    Tensions Influencing Global Foresight 8
    The Uses of Foresight 10
    Some Characteristics of Foresight 11
    Factors Promoting The Need and Demand For Foresight 11
    Factors Inhibiting The Demand For and The Use of Foresight 12

2 CONCEPTS AND PROCESSES OF ISSUES MANAGEMENT 15

    Conditions For Success 15
    Successful Practice 16
    Assumptions About Issues Management 18
    Issues as Conflicts 19
    Characteristics of an Emerging Issue 19
    Can You Anticipate Emerging Issues? 20
    Life Cycle of a Public Policy Issue 21
    Some Principles and Conditions For an Effective Issues
       Identification and Management Program .25
    Converting Principles to Practice 27
    Identifying The Emerging Issues: Scanning and Monitoring 30
    Some Approaches to Issues Identification 32
    Further Details on Issues Identification 36
    The Education Function 37
    Analytical and Interpretation Function 37
    Additional Considerations in Issues Management 38

Advice on Getting Started 39
An Alternative Point of View 43
Locating Issues Identification and Management In The
Organization 44

3   METHODS AND TECHNIQUES OF ISSUES MANAGEMENT 45

Introduction 45
Evaluation Factors 48
Some Additional Consideration 51
The Techniques 52
Technique: Networking 52
Technique: Precursor Analysis - Bellwether
Jurisdiction 54
Technique: Media Analysis (Column Inch Counting) 57
Technique: Polls and Surveys .59
Technique: Jury of Executive Opinion 62
Technique: Expert Panels 65
Technique: Scanning and Monitoring 66
Technique: Content Analysis 66
Technique: Legislative Tracking 68
Technique: Delphi 70
Technique: Conversational Delphi - The Structured
Interview 75
Technique: The Consensor 77
Technique: Cross Impact Analysis 78
Technique: Decision Support Systems 80
Technique: Computer Assisted Techniques 83
Technique: Small Group Processes 85
Technique: Scenario Building .87
Technique: Incidental Techniques of Some Use in
Issues Management 94
Technique: Techniques Not in General Use 95

4   ESTABLISHING AN ISSUES MANAGEMENT SYSTEM 97

Introduction 97
The Prototypical System 98
Step 1 - Diagnosis 98
Step 2 - Begin Small 98
Step 3 - Gradual Expansion 104
Making It All Work 105

5   A RESEARCH AGENDA 107

    The Role of Research in Issues Management 108
    The Priorities For Research 110
    Who Benefits From Issues Management Research 112
    Who Should Fund The Research 112
    Who Are The Researchers 112
    Observations and Comments On The Research Agenda 112
    Concluding Observations and Comments 114

Appendix A Further Acknowledgements 127
Bibliography 133
Index 139

PUBLISHER'S NOTE

We are pleased to present this book on *Issues Management*.

First, we believe that mounting a well-designed program of Issues Management is of vital importance to the long-term effectiveness of companies, government agencies, professional organizations and academic curricula. The combination of theory, analysis and technique in this book provides understanding and operational guidance—both of which are so essential to success.

Second, we are gratified to contribute to the dissemination of the ideas, values, wisdom and precepts of Joseph F. Coates, Vary T. Coates and their associates. Through research, consultation, teaching and inspiration the Coates' have provided exemplary leadership to the development of both theory and operational programs for three decades. They have sensitized and instructed private and public policy leaders throughout the world in objective assessment of the future as guidance for current policy decisions.

We share the Coates' precept that: "We have a moral obligation to be smart about the future."

Lowell H. Hattery
Publisher

PREFACE

Within the past decade issues management, a new form of futures research, has taken hold in corporate America. It is rapidly spreading to trade and professional associations and is beginning to be effectively applied in federal, state, and local government planning. *Issues management* is the organized activity of identifying emerging trends, concerns, or issues likely to affect an organization in the next few years and developing a wider and more positive range of organizational responses toward that future. Business and industry, in adopting issues management, seek to formulate creative alternatives to constraints, regulations, or confrontation. Often in the past, the awareness of a trend, a new development, or the possibility of new constraints came too late to frame anything but a reactive response.

In addition to the direct challenges to the organization, other factors in our increasingly complex society, such as changes in consumer behavior or in worker attitudes and performance, may result in new issues. Emerging issues may also affect access to raw materials and markets and have an effect on almost any other organizational activity.

Issues management as a skill or an art in planning is rapidly evolving and therefore lacks sharp boundaries on its scope, methods, or organizational setting. The purpose of issues identification and management is clear—to anticipate and identify unfolding trends and developments likely to have significant impact on the organization and to frame a positive response that serves the organization's needs in the new reality engendered by the trend or issue. The purpose of this book is to provide insights and information on how issues management has been used to identify, track, evaluate, and analyze emerging issues. This draws on three lines of investigation: review and evaluation of published documents and other literature; interviews and discussions with corporations, trade associations, government and other officials; detailed discussions with professional futurists and management specialists on particular techniques and processes.

The special study of issues management was carried out by J.F. Coates, Inc. under contract and support from the Electric Power Research Institute (EPRI). The book is largely the study report submitted to EPRI, supplemented by discussion of the setting of issues management within the framework of futures and foresight research.

The book is organized into four parts: background description of the concepts of futures research and issues management; methods and

techniques for issues management programs; guidelines for establishing an
issues management activity; and a research agenda on the process of issues
management.

   We believe the book to be useful to private and public decision-makers
and planners; to consultants to large organizations; to researchers in such
fields as forecasting, technology assessment, long-range planning and policy
making; and to professors and graduate students in public and business
management, economics and social planning, and other interdisciplinary
fields.

ACKNOWLEDGEMENTS

Credibility and quality control are essential components of the effective adoption of any new idea, concept, or study technique. To this end, the two projects from which this book is drawn have enjoyed the close cooperation of Sherman Feher, the project manager representing EPRI. In addition the advice and informal guidance of Gerald J. Edgley and Sue Lerner of the Edison Electric Institute have been helpful in this and earlier work connected with their industry and emerging issues.

A draft of the report, which comprises Chapters 2-4, enjoyed the benefit of a project review meeting. The participants included: Craig Conley and Michael Hertel of Southern California Edison; Sherman Feher and Monta Zengerle of EPRI; Paul Feldman of Pennsylvania Electric Company; Chuck Harvel of Public Service Company of New Mexico; Jim Lingle of Wisconsin Electric Power Company; Elmer Hildebrandt of the Detroit Edison Company; and Gerald Edgley of the Edison Electric Institute. The numerous issues managers, consultants, academics, vendors, and suppliers of services interviewed in connection with those chapters are acknowledged in Appendix A.

The material in Chapter 5 is drawn from a separate project for EPRI—Issues Identification and Management: Developing a Research Agenda. Again, grateful acknowledgement is made of the sponsor's role through Sherman Feher. The numerous contributors to that chapter in workshops or in interviews are also acknowledged in Appendix A.

Joseph F. Coates
President
J.F. Coates, Inc.

LOOKING TO THE FUTURE

Issues management is a means to assess the future and relate the findings to a specific organization or program. It is a subset of what is generally termed "futures research."

There are three reasons to study the future. First, it is fun. Second, it provides a base for personal, corporate, collective, and governmental planning. Third and most significantly, an effective look into the future provides us with an opportunity to control, to manage, or, at least, to influence that future.

Most, if not all, serious futurists share four fundamental propositions about the future. First, there are real alternative futures before us. Second, we can to a useful extent anticipate and picture what those futures may be. Third, we have the means to chart a course among those alternative futures rather than just drift in a tide of time and events. Fourth, we have the moral obligation to use these capabilities.

OUR WORLD HAS CHANGED

Another, quite different kind of reason for the study of the future is that the world has changed in fundamental ways, making obsolete many of the traditions, views, orientations, theories, and policies about the collective and social management of our public and private worlds.

Some 60 long-term trends are outlined in Table I. Together they constrain, define, and form the basis for our future. One can epitomize those changes in some brief statements. The most fundamental of these statements is that we in the United States today live in a totally man-made world. For the majority of us literally nothing that we ever encounter, whether in eating, sleeping, relaxing, or working, is not the product of man's enterprise. What is important about that is that we know very little about the stability, strength, resiliency, healing power, or forgiveness of that man-made world.

* This chapter draws on and contains excerpts from the following previously published materials by Joseph F. Coates: "Why Think About the Future: Some Administrative-Political Perspectives," *Public Administration Review*, September/October 1976; and Foresight in Federal Government Policymaking," *Futures Society Quarterly*, Summer 1985.

TABLE 1

LONG-TERM TRENDS FORMING THE BASIS FOR THE FUTURE

General Long-Term Societal Trends

1. Economic prosperity, affluence, and inflation
2. Expanding education throughout society
3. Rise of knowledge industries and a knowledge-dependent society
4. Relative decline in common knowledge of the physical world
5. Urbanization/metropolitanization/suburbanization
6. Rise of the middle class society
7. Cultural homogenization—the growth of a national society
8. Growth of permanent military establishment
9. Mobility, a) personal, b) physical, c) occupational, d) job
10. International affairs and national security as a major societal factor

Technology Trends

11. The centrality and increasing dominance of technology in the economy and society
12. Integration of the national economy
13. Integration of the national with the international economy
14. The growth of research and development as a factor in economy
15. High technological turnover rate
16. The development of mass media in telecommunications and printing
17. An awareness of the finitude of resources

Trends in Labor Force and Work

18. Specialization
19. Growth of the service sector
20. Relative decline of primary and secondary employment
21. Growth of information industries, movement toward an information society
22. Expansion of credentialism
23. Women, blacks, and other minority groups entering into the labor force
24. Early retirement
25. Unionism
26. Growth of pensions and pension funds
27. Movement toward second careers and midlife change in career
28. Decline of the work ethic

TABLE 1

LONG-TERM TRENDS FORMING THE BASIS FOR THE FUTURE
(Continued)

Trends in Values and Concerns

29. General shift in societal values
30. Diversity as a growing, explicit value
31. Decline of traditional authority
32. The growth of anti-authoritarian movements
33. Increasing aspirations and expectations of success
34. Growth of tourism, vacationing, and travel
35. General expectations of high level of medical care
36. General expectations of high level of social service
37. The growth of consumerism
38. Growth of physical culture and personal health movements
39. Civil rights, civil liberties expansion for blacks, Chicanos, gays, and other minorities
40. Growth of women's liberation movement

Family Trends

41. Decline in birth rates
42. Shifts in rates of family formation, marriage, divorce, and living styles
43. The growth of leisure
44. The growth of the do-it-yourself movement
45. Improved nutrition with the consequent decline in the age of menarche
46. Protracted adolescence
47. Decline in the number and significance of rites of passage, birth, death, marriage, etc.
48. Isolation of children from the world of adult concern
49. The acculturation of children by other children
50. The growth of a large aged population
51. The replacement of the extended family by the nuclear family and other living arrangements

Institutional Trends

52. The institutionalization of problems. This is the tendency to spawn new institutions and new institutional mechanisms for dealing with what were in the past personal, private, or nongovernmental responsibilities.
53. Bureaucratization of public and private institutions

TABLE 1

LONG-TERM TRENDS FORMING THE BASIS FOR THE FUTURE
(Continued)

54. Growth of big government
55. Growth of big business
56. Growth of multi-national corporations
57. Growth of future studies and forecasting and the institutionalization of foresight mechanisms and long-range planning.
58. Growth of public participation in public institution and private institution decision-making
59. The growing demands for accountability and the expenditure of public resources
60. Growth of demands for social responsibility

We know virtually nothing about that man-made world comparable to what a primitive man or a peasant knows about his world. Fundamentally, we do not understand enough about this world we have created in the last few decades and which we are continuing to rapidly expand and elaborate.

Technology, while known and found in every society of the world, is in the United States unique in its scale, its scope, its interrelatedness, its pervasiveness, its dollar investment, its rapid turnover, and its universal impact on every aspect of lives. This new role for technology has led us to what Daniel Bell calls the post-industrial society. That is not just a jargon term, but a fundamental conceptual theme that has to do with a basic shift in the structure of our society and economy. At the birth of the Republic, the bulk of the work force was in agriculture. In the 19th and early 20th centuries industry was dominant. About 15 years ago labor made a transition predominately into services. That does not reveal the more basic fact about American society—that a large share of working Americans, perhaps as little as 45 and as much as 55 percent, now deal with the new dominant commodity in society. The dominant commodity is not corn or grain or agricultural products or petroleum. It is not automobiles, housing, or transportation. The dominant commodity of American society is information. Science, as the source of knowledge, is becoming the new central driver in American society.

A fundamental, ironic, and intrinsic feature of new knowledge is that it automatically generates new ignorance. The more striking the new knowledge, the more fundamental its ramifications, the wider and deeper the pool of ignorance which it generates. Consider, for example, development in telecommunications, nuclear energy, and genetics in the past three decades. The systematic exploration of the future is more and more urgent as our competence expands.

TECHNOLOGICAL BLUNDERS

Many major and minor technological projects and developments have resulted in undesirable and often unexpected side effects. Many of these, by the nature of the case, would have been difficult to anticipate. However, there are numerous cases in which it is clear that foresight could have been exercised, and that foresight could have led to more socially desirable outcomes. Some examples are:

1. The Aswan High Dam, which, having been completed, is observed to be silting, and to have promoted propagation of snails and the associated disease, bilharzia. The dam has reduced the nutrients flowing to the Mediterranean, which in turn led to the decline of the fish catch. The failure to irrigate the lands of Egypt annually is creating a demand for artificial fertilizers. The artificial lake created by the dam is plagued by pest vegetation.

2. A California state official announced there was a deficit of kindergarten children. This clearly is a reflection of the failure to integrate available demographic data into planning.

3. The overproduction of certain categories of professional workers, such as school teachers and lawyers, is something which could have been brought into better balance by greater social and institutional awareness of long-term trends and activities in schools and in employment.

4. The pollution problems resulting from the growth of large numbers of automobiles in urban areas was a fully predictable consequence of the physical characteristics of automobiles.

5. The expansion of cities into rich suburban farmlands, and the associated change in agricultural production, local industry, and land uses, were all generally predictable.

The fact that we have so many diverse evidences of apparently unnecessary excessive side effects should alert the decision-makers in and out of government to the potential for doing our business in a newer and better way.

GREATER RISKS

As noted earlier, new knowledge intrinsically generates ignorance about its consequences. Therefore, planning in and for the future must be on the basis of an increasingly richer mix of uncertainty and certainty in technological, economic, and social analysis.

Many risks are greater now as new technology propagates rapidly through society, because of the high degree of economic, commercial, social, and institutional networking which facilitates the introduction and spread of innovation. Consequently, the traditionally effective means used in the past, i.e., trying things out in the market on a small scale and moving ahead slowly, is no longer feasible or practical. The damage that can be done can be too great. A classic example is thalidomide and the wave of phocomelic children which resulted from its use.

In other cases, technology carries intrinsic risks of such uncertainty that we do not know how to deal with them at any given time. An example is the interaction of fluorocarbons with the ozone of the stratosphere. A more chronic and continuing case is that of nuclear power plant waste. This increasing scope, scale, and integration of risk into society demands more foresight and long-range planning.

In some cases, the risk is not necessarily environmental or social, but may be institutional, organizational, and financial. An interesting example of this situation, calling for extended future studies, is in forest products. Forests grow on a cycle of 20 to 100 years. Consequently people in the forestry, lumber, paper and pulp business must have effective long-range planning in order to assure their business future. Similarly in the utility industry, with a seven to 15 year cycle from initiation to opening of a new facility, one must intrinsically, not accidentally, plan on a decades time-scale. Virtually any technology which has a long startup time and a long life automatically drives one to long-range planning and a deeper consideration of the future.

THE AVAILABILITY OF INSTITUTIONAL AND
PERSONNEL RESOURCES FOR FUTURE STUDIES

One of the great myths in the American society is that there is extensive and widespread long-range planning in both government and business. Aside from the rare cases of civil works, military strategic and logistics planning, and the rather unique case of NASA, there is almost no long-range planning in government. In the business community, considering the Fortune 500 corporations, there are perhaps no more than a few dozen that are prominent in the area of true long-term planning. Most business decisions are made on a one to five-year planning horizon. Consequently, although there is a substantial cadre of people in planning functions, their horizons are foreshortened and inappropriate for dealing with our new complexities. On the other hand, we have learned to institutionalize long-range future forecasting in a number of ways which could have a major beneficial effect on society.

Some of the most interesting developments in institutionalizing futures are occurring on Capitol Hill. The Congressional Research Service has formed a Futures Study Group. The House of Representatives has passed the foresight provision which requires, under House Rule 988, X, 2. (B) (1), that each standing committee, other than Budget and Appropriations, "shall on a continuing basis undertake futures research and forecasting on matters within the jurisdiction of that committee." Congress has also moved to further expand its competence in analytical and support studies, service, and public policy, through the formation of the Office of Technology Assessment and the Congressional Budget Office. For the executive side of government there has been spawned a number of public, private, profit and non-profit, large and small futures study groups, ranging from the Rand Corporation and the Stanford Research Institute to numerous universities, future study centers, and private groups such as the Institute for the Future and The Futures Group. Data periodically collected indicates that some 200 institutions are engaged in these activities to a substantial extent as part of their business. Perhaps the most interesting single measure of the expansion of the futures field is the growth of the World Future Society from its inception in 1966 to its present membership of 25,000. The study of the future is also moving down into the state and local levels of government, as well as moving across the agencies at the federal level.

SERIOUS FUTURISM

I find it convenient to make a distinction between serious futurists and those who are merely earnest. Those who are earnest tend too often to be polemicists, doomsayers, ideologically motivated, with a strong publicist sense, often playing to the grandstand or engaging in consciousness raising. Their analyses often present exciting, newsworthy, but unbalanced assessments of the future. The earnest but not serious futurist often neglects to test the flexibility of the system and tends to neglect the political-institutional options ahead of us. Serious futurism tends to relate public, private, governmental, corporate, and institutional policies to a context of issues, options, and alternatives.

Finally, the fun element in the study of futures ought not be overlooked. If you do not enjoy the game element in it you are either doing it wrong or are not cut out for the work.

A product of futures research is foresight. Foresight is the overall process of creating an understanding and appreciation of information generated by looking ahead. Foresight includes qualitative and quantitative means for monitoring clues and indicators of evolving trends and developments, and is best and most useful when directly linked to the analysis of policy implications. Foresight prepares us to meet the needs and opportunities of the future. Foresight in government cannot define policy, but it can help condition policies to be more appropriate, more flexible, and more robust in their implementation, as times and circumstances change. Foresight is, therefore, closely tied to planning. It is not planning—merely a step in planning. Some characteristics of an institutionalized system of foresight for planning are that:

- The process must be systematic and comprehensive, drawing upon as wide a scope of information as is appropriate to the subject under consideration.

- The process must be able to accommodate a wide range of information of varying degrees of credibility, completeness, and technical and scientific soundness.

- The process must be public, at least in the minimal sense that the assumptions, the mechanisms by which conclusions are drawn, and the data and information drawn upon must be available for independent scrutiny, analysis, and evaluation.

- The best foresight activities avoid prediction, that is, any conclusive or probabilistic statement that particular events will or will not occur. Foresight attempts to fan out a full range of alternative developments compatible with alternative assumptions and the quality of the data.

TENSIONS INFLUENCING ORGANIZATIONAL FORESIGHT

Unfortunately, a number of tensions are built into the search for better foresight which preclude any ready or definitive remedy.

- **Expanding Needs Conflict with the Constraints on Acquiring New Knowledge.** The need of policy makers for new knowledge is without limit. Each new body of knowledge seems to create demand for further knowledge. Each new tool demands its extension to some new limit. Furthermore, the required data are not always available, easily collected, or cheap. In addition, converting data into knowledge through analysis, understanding, and presentation is often slow and expensive.

- **Pressure for Action Conflicts with the Uncertainty of Outcomes.** While policy decisions can be deferred, sooner or later the move to action is called for and must always be made in the context of uncertainties about the success of the policy or plan and the outcome of the actions thereby triggered.

- **Rapid Change and Increasing Complexity Conflict with Our Limited Human Ability to Think about Large Numbers of Factors Simultaneously.** A tendency, therefore, is to oversimplify complex situations or to use aids such as mathematical modeling to increase our insight into complexity. While oversimplification often enters into the analysis of extremely complex situations, a further simplification is likely to occur as the results of a foresight activity are briefed and transmitted from person to person in ever diminishing detail.

- **The Pressure for Quick Response Conflicts with the Needs for More Data.** Every issue involves data and every analysis calls for data. Consequently, a general policy is to anticipate data needs and to gather and stockpile data. Where one does not have it fully in hand one often makes more or less wise estimates. Data and time, however, also come in conflict in that it takes time to act and, in turn, time for responses to develop from actions. Consequently, foresight requires the continuing collection of data with regard to past and new actions, in order to determine their consequences and to put us in better shape for managing the future.

- **Preference for Quantitative Data and Mathematical Analysis is at Odds with the Need for Some Qualitative Data and Subjective Evaluation.** Numbers have a purported degree of reliability, validity, and public character that make them the preferred policy coinage. But the underlying significance of the numbers is often obscure and often tells only part of a complex story. Often the most critical policy aspects of a potential development or venture hinge upon what can only be described in conjectural, "what if" or discursive fashion, such as the likelihood of the participation of the key actor, the uncertain interaction of complex social or political variables, or the poorly understood points of weakness in a potential venture.

- **The Need for Efficiency and Effectiveness Conflicts with the Need for Flexibility.** The need to allow alternative forms of analysis to flourish is very important in policy research. Striking a balance between centralization which promises efficiency and effectiveness on the one hand, and flexibility on the other, is difficult. Useful analysis requires alternative approaches to be explored simultaneously.

- **Science as a Rational Process Often Conflicts with Ideological and Political Factors.** The attempts to make policy analyses scientific, objective, and rational clash with practical constraints of ideology and the practical realities of political judgment. The risk of centralized analyses in a politically charged environment is that ideology and politics may too often swamp knowledge and objectivity.

- **The Short-Term Factors are Almost Always in Conflict with the Long-Term Factors.** Every decision-maker, public and private, elected and appointed, is continually beleaguered by short-term pressures for action even though he may know that longer-term outcomes and actions to shape the future may be more important.

- **The Pressure for Certainty is in Conflict with the Contingent and Hypothetical.** Good policy analysis, whether involving quantitative or qualitative techniques, must continually face the question of "What if?" and must continually traffic in "Let us suppose" information and data. These needs are particularly at odds with rigid organizations, bureaucracy, narrow specialization, and ideological preconception.

THE USES OF FORESIGHT

Among the readily recognized uses of foresight, in both public and private institutions, are the following:

- to explore the effects of extending current policies;

- to widen the range of choices regarding current policy and to clarify their possible consequences;

- to provide early warning about potential or normally unanticipated difficulties;

- to provide an early alert to potential new opportunities;

- to test the consistency of a policy, both internally and with regard to other policies;

- to provide a context for planning (this is a particularly common use of foresight in the corporation, where the changing world outside the immediate authority of the corporation is having an increasingly significant effect on its operations);

- to explore unlikely but highly significant or seriously disruptive developments (the so-called wild cards); and

- to suggest the appropriate focus for economic, technical, social, environmental, or other monitoring and research.

It is important to distinguish between foresight, forecasting, and modeling:

- Foresight can be taken to be a process by which one comes to a fuller understanding of the forces shaping the long-term future which should be taken into account in policy formulation, planning, and decision-making.

- Forecasting is a generic term for methods or techniques in estimating the future situation, based generally on a systematic analysis of historical and current data. Forecasting is sometimes quantitative, often qualitative.

- A model is a representation of a system or process showing interacting elements.

SOME CHARACTERISTICS OF FORESIGHT

Foresight is a process, not a technique. As a process, foresight not only uses techniques such as modeling, it uses consultative processes and aggressively seeks feedback. As an organizational process, foresight works in the service of decision-making and the clarification of choices. Consequently, the process must effectively feed into decision-making institutions and to decision-makers. The foresight process must also flow out to affected and concerned parties in order to sharpen its analysis, test its conclusions, and further define the quality and significance of its conclusions.

Foresight cannot occur in an organizational vacuum; each of the elements of the process must be located somewhere. The locus of foresight is the core of much of the present public discussion, and will be expanded on below.

Foresight and forecasting are art forms. They are not sciences although they may draw upon any of the sciences. Contemporary forecasting makes extensive use of mathematical modeling.

FACTORS PROMOTING THE NEED AND DEMAND FOR FORESIGHT

At least five factors push toward more attention to the future:

- The growing awareness of the increasing complexity of our world and the accelerating pace of change, each of which can raise the cost of a false step.

- The awareness that the mental models, that is, the images of the world with which many people operate, are vague, uncertain, plastic, and not clearly stated. Any techniques which clarify those mental models will be a step ahead.

- Computer assisted mathematical modeling took a major jump ahead with the development of large so-called mainframe computers and is now taking a second major leap ahead with the widespread proliferation of microcomputers. This gives large numbers of people and vast numbers of organizations the capability to manipulate, manage, and model data, and also to test, question, evaluate, and challenge government and private models and modeling efforts.

- Fear stimulates an interest in foresight: fear of mismanagement of technological projects; fear of the adverse effects of thoughtless, impetuous, or unplanned action; fear that the environment is less capable of accommodating our mistakes.

- There are widely held beliefs of causal connections between much of what goes on in our world, including much of social and human behavior. Efforts at foresight are part of a wider search for theories of social and technological change.

FACTORS INHIBITING THE DEMAND FOR AND THE USE OF FORESIGHT

A number of serious considerations and legitimate concerns are inhibitors to the adoption of foresight tools and processes. These factors flow from previous bad experiences, the intellectual and practical limitations on foresight, and the need to balance factors in public administration. For example:

- There is widespread fear that institutionalized foresight can easily become doctrinaire foresight, hence stifling innovation and the exploration of alternatives which have been strengths of our political and economic system.

- Attempts to exercise foresight, when begun too late, can end up being misleading by being too little or too late in the decision cycle.

- The institutionalization of foresight, some fear, will promote central government planning. Foresight by widening the span of considerations entering into decisions draws things together conceptually. This may lead to centralization of control or approval of public and private action.

- Foresight may create organizational confusion by introducing conflicting or useless signals into the decision process, raising matters of concern which are outside the scope of the user's responsibilities or formulating options which delay but do not contribute to the final outcome.

Acting today to create a better tomorrow calls for maps and pointers to the many directions the future may take.

Four assumptions should guide work in futures and foresight research: the alternatives ahead of us are real; we can anticipate future developments to a degree that is useful to planning; we can act to encourage the desirable and to discourage the undesirable; we have a moral obligation to be smart about the future.

2

CONCEPTS AND PROCESSES OF ISSUES MANAGEMENT

Issues management is the orchestrating of a positive plan for dealing with issues, rather than merely reacting to them. It is a tool now used in corporations and trade associations to come to an earlier and more constructive understanding of the issues an organization or industry will face in the next few years. Based on interviews with issues managers, people in the electric utility industry, and other practitioners and observers, we have identified key considerations in assessing the conditions under which issues management could be an effective support system for senior executives. The report offers a generic model of issues management based upon collective information to date.

Issues management offers new advantages in planning and managing for an uncertain future. It can make an organization an active participant in shaping its future, rather than a reactive victim of inadequately considered legislative and regulatory responses to problems.

Issues management as an organizational process does three things:

- Identifies, monitors and analyzes social, technological, political, and economic forces and trends which will affect an industry or an organization.

- Interprets and defines implications and options. The earlier the situation is understood, the wider in scope and the more positive these options may be.

- Sets in motion the shorter and longer term operational and strategic actions to deal with the situation. By anticipating issues, an organization increases its opportunities to formulate a strategy that supports and enhances its long-range goals.

CONDITIONS FOR SUCCESS

To be successful issues management must:

- Be tailored to the corporate culture and management dynamics of the organization.

- Enjoy the full active commitment of top executives.

- Be implemented gradually and build a constituency in operating units by helping them.

- Seek and achieve broad participation at the operating and staff levels.

SUCCESSFUL PRACTICE

The benefits of issues management depend on the practices below becoming regular, continuing activities:

- Scanning, harvesting, and collating information, clues, and indicators from many sources such as newspapers, magazines, journals, professional and lay publications, broadcast media, documents, and personal networks.

- Monitoring of selected trends and emerging issues systematically with periodic reanalysis and interpretation.

- Interpreting this material by and with senior managers to reveal credible potential outcomes with significant possible consequences for the organization's well-being.

- Determining options and selecting actions to reduce any threats and to enhance the benefits implicit in unfolding events.

- Regularly using open channels to and from senior executives to inform them about emerging issues and to evoke their involvement.

- Achieving voluntary participation by and input from people at all levels, and recognizing and rewarding their involvement.

- Delivering fully interpreted and easily grasped information useful to operating divisions and senior managers.

- Maintaining a network of both internal and external sources of information, interpretation, and advice.

- Sorting, winnowing, interpreting, clarifying and reducing the burden of issues information reaching decision-makers and others.

Many techniques are used in issues management, ranging from simple, low-cost scanning and preliminary analysis methods to sophisticated, computer-assisted data storage and analysis tools. The proper choice depends on the organizational culture and style of decision-making, the perception of the significance of the external environment, and the enthusiasm of top managers for involvement. These techniques are described, analyzed, and evaluated in Chapter 3.

Many terms are used for activities which are now generally called "Issues Management" or "Issues Identification and Management." The concept, insofar as it is a new future oriented policy and planning tool, and insofar as it involves practice across many kinds of organizations, businesses, industries, and trade associations, is still evolving in terminology, technique, scope, and organizational setting. It has recently emerged as a tool in federal, state, and local government planning. It as yet has no sharp and definitive boundaries. There is a great deal of exploration, probing of techniques, and trial and error in strategies for institutionalizing whatever processes may be tried. Consequently, in the absence of fixed boundaries as to what issues management is, we must begin by understanding the situation to which it is a response, and by tracing out the alternative forms in which issues management evolves.

Issues management frequently uses the term "environment." In that context the term refers not merely to the natural and man-made physical environment, but to the whole external situation in which the activities of an organization are embedded. Environment includes social and attitudinal changes, technological developments, political and public administrative trends, matters of domestic and international trade and commerce, and a variety of other developing concerns which could influence the raw materials, markets, labor force, products and services, and any other aspect of an organization's functions.

With the expanding growth and complexity of the U.S. economy and society following World War II, the rise in general education and prosperity, the shift away from the Depression and war to expansion and growth, and the new emphasis on amenities and quality of life, our society gradually became attentive to the unwanted side effects of industrial and business developments. As one result, the past 25 years have seen an unprecedented growth in federal legislation and bureaucratic regulation, reflecting these widening public concerns and stemming from effective political action by public interest groups. Often a business organization's response to these trends, in the two to three decades immediately following World War II, was a combination of denial, indignation, defensiveness, and resistance.

Negative response to this ever expanding range of public concerns, however effective it may have been in the short run, proved to be a deficient strategy in longer run. Organizations are increasingly taking not a damage-limiting but an opportunity-expanding stance in response to broad social concerns.

ASSUMPTIONS ABOUT ISSUES MANAGEMENT

Issues management is a new approach and a new strategy with regard to these unfolding issues. It assumes that:

- Issues can be identified earlier and more fully and reliably than they have been in the past.

- Early anticipation widens the range of choices open to organizations.

- Early anticipation allows time for an organization to study the issue, understand its choices, understand the role of various actors, and identify a fuller range of technical, social, economic, and other variables entering into the situation.

- Earlier awareness permits the organization, in many cases, to assume a positive rather than a negative orientation toward an emerging issue.

- The organization will early, rather than late, seek out and meet with the concerned parties, some of whom were heretofore not known to them as having a stake in the issue, or were known only as hostile antagonists.

- The organization can begin early and positively to supply information to legislators, regulators, bureaucrats, and other interested and influential publics, to give them a more realistic understanding of the issue and feasible responses.

With this complex of objectives and a new strategic approach to issues, it should be clear that no full-blown, fully effective program or set of techniques will spring up overnight.

Issues identification and management is plausible because emerging issues are the consequences of changes in the society, the economy, public attitudes, education, new scientific knowledge, and technological developments that can be observed and even anticipated. Because many changes are occurring simultaneously in our complex world, it is not easy to identify and sort out the important changes and effectively anticipate the impacts they will have. Currently, issues management is principally an activity of large corporations; it is not yet generally practiced in mid-size and small organizations. Issues identification has however become an increasingly important activity of trade and professional associations.

ISSUES AS CONFLICTS

Issues management primarily deals with conflicts of interests or values, not with problems, which can in theory have definitive answers or solutions. This distinction is extremely important in understanding the origins and strategies for dealing with issues. There may be a tendency, particularly in some technology-based organizations, to interpret every difficulty as a problem, that is, a matter fully tractable to the application of expert knowledge and other resources. The tendency is to downplay, or even deny, deep-seated, lasting, and insoluble conflicts associated with its activities, or to re-interpret those conflicts as problems. The difficulties with the problem format as the way of coping with issues are that, first, it cannot lead to resolution of the issues as long as competing values remain; and, second, it leads to a great deal of wasted motion and resources in failing to deal with the submerged conflict.

Conflicts can arise over technological choices; and they can arise over divergent interests between an organization and its workforce, its consumers, or other parties that it affects indirectly. Conflicts can arise between short-term pressures and long-term goals. The essential characteristic of a conflict or issue is that it almost never can be definitively and completely resolved to the full satisfaction of all parties, but instead some dynamic balance in interests, or mutual accommodation, must be sought. Negotiation, compromise, trade-offs and exchanges often mark the successful management of an issue, whereas problems may be solved by the application of additional information.

There are no hard and fast rules about the time horizon to be used in issues management. We have generally used "short-term" or "immediate" to apply to issues that have already engaged the organization's attention, or that will be forced on the management's attention within the next two years. Some argue that the most immediate problems should not be included in issues management because it is too late to do much constructive about them. Issues that will come into full force during the next three to five years, the most important focus of issues management, we have called intermediate term issues. Long-term issues are those that will ripen in five to ten years, or even longer.

CHARACTERISTICS OF AN EMERGING ISSUE

In general, an emerging issue has six characteristics making its early identification particularly important to each of the actors involved in its long-term resolution:

- The terms of the debate can not yet be clearly defined.

- One of the actors will define the emerging issue and make it a current issue.

- It deals with matters of conflicting values and interest.

- It is not a problem that expert knowledge will automatically be able to resolve.

- It is stated in value-laden terms.

- Trade-offs are possible across categories.

Lacking a clear-cut definition, by virtue of being "emerging," and having many diffuse tentacles into a variety of related matters, the issue in its early stages can usually be stated only in somewhat general terms. Yet how the issue is defined to a large extent determines the recruitment of support and ultimately defines the temper and content of legislative, regulatory, and courtroom resolution. For example, characterizing a labor issue as "right to work" creates an orientation to the issue. In the contemporary issues of abortion, the very terminology of "right to life" or "pro-choice" influences one's orientation toward the issue.

It is also worth noting that seldom are the trade-offs involved in the resolution of an issue in comparable categories. Consequently, a full understanding of the issue involves understanding all the actors and the options, issues, goals, and incentives entering into their decision framework.

CAN YOU ANTICIPATE EMERGING ISSUES?

The answer is an unequivocal "yes." Some issues have been anticipated and effectively dealt with. One need not claim that all issues can be identified years in advance. One needs only to accept the more limited proposition that a useful number of unfolding issues can be identified early enough to justify the time, labor, and expense of a formal organizational process. The measure of "worthwhile" is that the organization is in a better position than it would have been without an institutionalized alerting function.

The most unequivocal evidence that emerging issues can be identified, and that the process is worthwhile, is that many organizations are doing issues management. Among those organizations most generally recognized as having active issues management capability in the private and public sector and in trade associations are the following:

Fortune 500 Companies

- AT&T
- ARCO (Atlantic Richfield Co.)
- PPG Industries
- Pitney Bowes
- Monsanto Corporation
- Sears Roebuck & Co.
- Sperry Rand
- Westinghouse
- General Electric Co.
- United Airlines

Trade Organizations

- National Association
  of Manufacturers
- The Conference Board

Non-profit Organizations

- United Way

Government Agencies

- Office of Technology Assessment, U.S. Congress
- U.S. General Accounting Office
- Congressional Research Service, Library of Congress
- Environmental Protection Agency
- Congressional Clearinghouse on the Future

These, and other organizations interviewed in connection with this report, have now made issues management a standard and routine part of their activity.

From a theoretical point of view, the Harvard sociologist Daniel Bell has pointed out that " . . . [what is] social today becomes political tomorrow, and economic [in costs and consequences] the day after." Reginald H. Jones, retired Chief Executive Officer (CEO) at General Electric, is more trenchant in his acknowledgment of the role of emerging issues: "Public policy and social issues are not peripheral to business planning and management today: today, they are the mainstream of it."

Let us turn to the question of whether there are usefully repeating patterns that should guide an issues management process.

LIFE CYCLE OF A PUBLIC POLICY ISSUE

The National Association of Manufacturers, particularly in the conceptualizations by Dr. Jane Work, has taken Daniel Bell's concept and defined a life cycle of public policy (see Figure 2-1).

In broad terms, the development stage, the early emerging issues stage, is when an early warning system and monitoring are most effective in identifying the felt needs and dissatisfactions of those who will become the

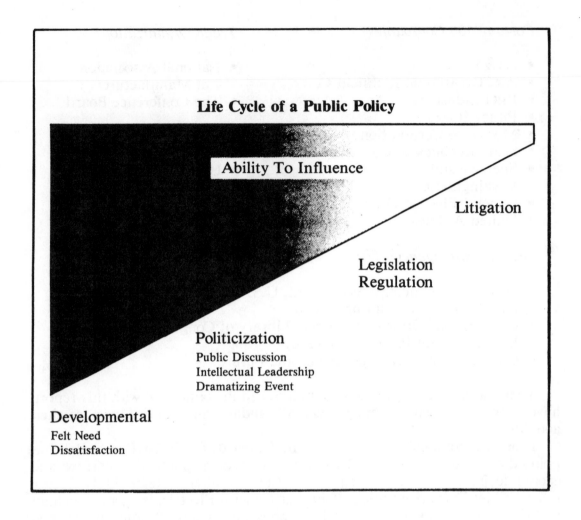

Figure 2-1. Life Cycle of a Public Policy

Source: National Association of Manufacturers, "The Public Policy Process-
         Part One: Shaping Future Agendas, *"Perspective on National
         Issues*, June 1984, p. 2.

relevant actors. The issue, then, moves through a politicization stage of
public discussion; existing or new intellectual leadership comes forward, and
dramatic effects occur which underline the issue. The now fully emerged
issue moves into the legislative or regulatory cycle, and from there to
litigation and clarification. It finally settles into a stable part of the corporate
planning context. Note the core observation in Dr. Work's diagram that, with
the passage of time through the life cycle of the issue, the organization's
room for maneuvering steadily decreases. Therefore, while many of the issues

at the early stages only "could" affect the organization, it is essential to monitor them, because should the organization have to respond later, its influence will diminish while the issue matures and it will remain oblivious, indifferent, or ignorant of the emerging conflict.

A more detailed and fine-grained historical perspective on emerging issues has been presented by Edward Lawless in his groundbreaking book, *Technology and Social Shock*. Based on fifty cases of emerging public concerns about technology, he has proposed a generic time line in the development of an emerging issue derived from a scientific or technological development (Figure 2-2).

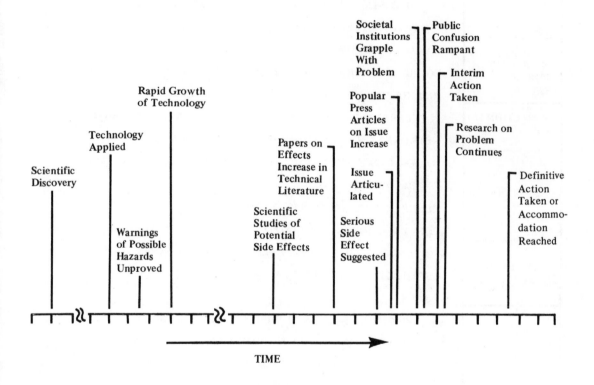

Figure 2-2. Time Line of an Emerging Technology-based Issue

Source: From *Technology and Social Shock* by Edward W. Lawless.
Copyright © 1977 by Rutgers, the State University of New Jersey.

From a quite different perspective, Graham Molitor offers a ten-phase life cycle of emerging issues, which provides direct guidance as to where to begin the process of early identification (Figure 2-3).

VISIONARY UNINHIBITED	—ARTISTIC, POETIC WORKS . . . .
	—SCIENCE FICTION . . . .
	—FRINGE MEDIA, UNDERGROUND PRESS . . . .
RENDERING IDEA TO SPECIFICS	—UNPUBLISHED NOTES AND SPEECHES . . . .
	—MONOGRAPHS, TREATISES . . . .
CORROBORA-TION OF DETAILS	—SCIENTIFIC, TECHNICAL, PROFESSIONAL JOURNALS . . . .
	—HIGHLY SPECIALIZED, NARROW-VIEWPOINT JOURNALS . . . .
	—STATISTICAL DOCUMENTS (SOCIAL INDICATORS, STATISTICAL SERVICES) . . . .
	—ABSTRACTING SERVICES, JOURNALS . . . .
DIFFUSION OF AN IDEA AMONG OPINION LEADERS	—DATASEARCH COMPOSITES (PREDICAST) . . . .
	—EGGHEAD JOURNALS (e.g., SCIENCE, SCIENTIFIC AMERICAN) . . . . . .
	—INSIDER "DOPESHEETS" (e.g., PRODUCT SAFETY LETTER) . . . .
INSTITUTIONAL RESPONSE	—POPULAR INTELLECTUAL MAGAZINES (e.g., HARPERS, ATLANTIC) . . . .
	—NETWORK COMMUNICATIONS (BULLETINS, NEWSLETTERS) . . . .
MASS MEDIA	—JOURNALS FOR THE CAUSE (e.g., CONSUMER REPORTS, ASBESTOS REPORTER) . . . .
	—GENERAL INTEREST PUBLICATIONS (e.g., TIME, NEWSWEEK) . . . .
	—CONDENSATION OF GENERAL LITERATURE (e.g., READER'S DIGEST) . .
POLITICIZING THE ISSUE	—POLL DATA, PUBLIC OPINION, BEHAVIORAL AND VOTER ATTITUDES . .
	—LEGISLATIVE/GOVERNMENTAL SERVICES, REPORTS . . . .
	—BOOKS
	—FICTION – NOVELS PROVIDE SOCIAL ANALYSES OF THE TIMES . .
	—NON-FICTION – PULL TOGETHER DISCORDANT PARTS INTO EASILY UNDERSTOOD WHOLE . . . .
INSTANTANEOUS COVERAGE FOR MASS CONSUMPTION	—NEWSPAPERS (NEW YORK TIMES & WASHINGTON POST EARLY, SOUTHERN RURAL PAPERS LATE COMMENTATORS) . . . .
	—RADIO & TELEVISION (NETWORKS COMMENT EARLER THAN LOCAL STATIONS) . . . .
EDUCATING THE PEOPLE TO THE NEW NORM	—EDUCATION JOURNALS . . . .
HISTORICAL ANALYSIS	—HISTORICAL ANALYSES . . . .
	—TRADITIONAL DOCTORAL THESES . . . .

Figure 2-3. Identifying Emerging Issues

Source: Personal communication with Graham Molitor of Public Policy
      Forecasting, Inc.

SOME PRINCIPLES AND CONDITIONS FOR AN EFFECTIVE ISSUES IDENTIFICATION AND MANAGEMENT PROGRAM

Collective corporate experience to date makes it clear that an issues management program is not seen as an obvious and necessary adjunct to management and planning in every corporation. The essential condition for starting such a program is:

- The corporation has experienced directly and at some significant cost one or more unexpected involvements in a public issue, or it sees other companies much like itself having experienced such travail. In contrast, organizations that tend to be market focused and that have had relatively few or only readily manageable public involvements and no problems in coping with regulations and legislation look at this early attention to mid-range future planning considerations as of minor importance.

The attention, support, active endorsement, and participation of top management is essential.

- Depending on the organizational culture, the initiation of an issues management program can begin with the top person or one or more members of the Executive Committee or Board of Directors. In other organizations, senior to middle management advocacy is often necessary to lay the groundwork and prepare the senior management for this initiative. There is no unequivocal rule as to how the enthusiasm begins; what is unequivocal is that for issues management to work, top management must be involved and committed.

Historically, the process has begun in one of several places. More often than not, it is begun in a public affairs office or a related office. But as the importance of issues management becomes more prominent, the trend has been to draw it closer and closer to the CEO or at least to the Executive Committee.

- A program cannot succeed if it merely feeds information to other staff, operating personnel, or senior management.

- An effective process must have broad internal participation and support. Those involved must understand how the process of identification, tracking, and monitoring works; where their own participation will be effective; how information is used; and must be continually and frequently reinforced about the effectiveness of the program.

- While it is not always practical, the program should, wherever possible, be a measure of annual performance or be made a factor in the annual performance rating for middle and senior managers.

Issues management is not an independent process but must be integrated into other key functions.

- The integration of issues management is forward into strategic planning, backward into operational planning. In many organizations issues management is a central function, while in others, it has gone through that phase and has proven to be more effective when decentralized into operating units, whether to departments, divisions, or companies. The details of where responsibility lies have to do with the degree of diversity in the corporation, its size, and a series of factors connected with the culture and customs of the organization.

The scope of the process is quite important.

- The process must be comprehensive in finding all the potential emerging issues, and complemented by a mechanism for setting priorities among the issues. Setting priorities must involve specific criteria, specific accountability of responsibility for the selection, and specific responsibilities for follow-through.

One cannot get away with merely the general; the issues must be tied to specific corporate and managerial concerns.

- One of the recurrent problems in issues identification and management is tieing broad social change, such as changing patterns in the workforce, integration of women into the workplace, or emerging concerns about toxic trace materials in the natural environment to specific corporate concerns. Managers cannot deal with the general. However important the general trend might be, it must be made operationally significant. That specification of issues, in terms of the corporate interest, is perhaps the single most difficult task in dealing with emerging issues.

Issues management cannot treat everything as of equal importance.

- The process of issues management must eventually yield specific priorities and have operational or strategic implications.

Issues management must draw on external sources and must therefore have mechanisms for outreach.

- There would be little need for issues identification were the internal resources of the organization adequate to deal with all its problems. Therefore, if the discussion of issues and the strategy for dealing with them is left totally to internal staff, the issue will surely drift out of focus. Processes must involve some attempt at external validation, whether through external data gathering, collective industry action, or some other method.

From issues identification through the move toward planning and management, the KISS principle is profoundly important—Keep It Simple, Stupid. Derivative of that:

- The process must be kept in perspective.

CONVERTING PRINCIPLES TO PRACTICE

Meeting the general objectives of issues management, namely the early and timely identification of emerging problems and the conversion of that awareness into some kind of significant managerial actions, can be extremely complex. The first cut at identifying the stages of that process is shown in Figure 2-4, drawn from the National Association of Manufacturers' report on perspectives on national issues. (Similar processes are used by Shell, Allied Chemical, Allstate, United Airlines, and other corporations.) This schema defines the high points in a complex process. It has, however, the intrinsic deficiency of not showing the alternative pathways and feedback associated with the actual implementation of an issues management process. A somewhat more comprehensive version of the same material is shown in Figure 2-5.

In considering Figure 2-5, assume that there is an issues management system in place. One of the key elements is a scanning function, which involves some mechanism for broadly sweeping the universe of potentially available information inside and outside the organization for developments, trends, issues, factors, and forces which could affect some important aspect of the organization's operation. Those aspects might be supplies, raw materials, labor, markets, new products, or new concerns with regard to products. Those effects and forces might come out of social, economic, political, technological, scientific, biological, ecological, international, or other developments.

A second key element, complementing the scanning, is monitoring, a more refined and detailed kind of information search reflecting the fact that the scanning process and the subsequent analytical and evaluation procedures have already identified certain topics as potentially important. Those specific topics are candidates for more detailed and continuing monitoring. Whereas scanning, which is open ended, might cover hundreds

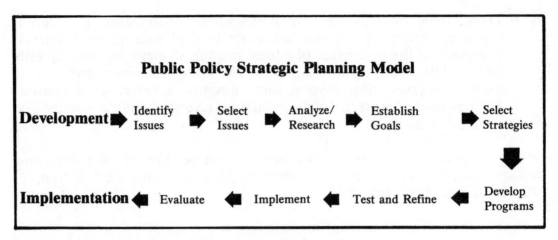

Figure 2-4. Public Policy Strategic Planning Model

Source: National Association of Manufacturers, "The Public
        Policy Process-Part One: Shaping Future Agendas,"
        Perspective on National Issues, 1984, p. 4.

of actual or potential topics, monitoring is likely to be limited to at most a
few dozen topics. The results of the monitoring and scanning feed into some
kind of analytical process, which organizationally may be centralized or
decentralized.

    That analytical function must:

- Define and redefine the short-, mid-, and long-term implications of
  these new developments for the organization.

- Identify or make assignments for the identification of further detailed
  background material.

- Look for implications for the organization and perhaps for the
  industry.

- Begin a rough-cut analysis of the implications and potential responses,
  whether those responses involve shifts in products, sites, manufacturing
  procedures, safety, legislative outreach, public relations and public
  affairs actions, or anything else that the organization may do.

- Feed back into monitoring to add new topics, or drop old ones from
  the list.

- Focus sharply on what is to be monitored.

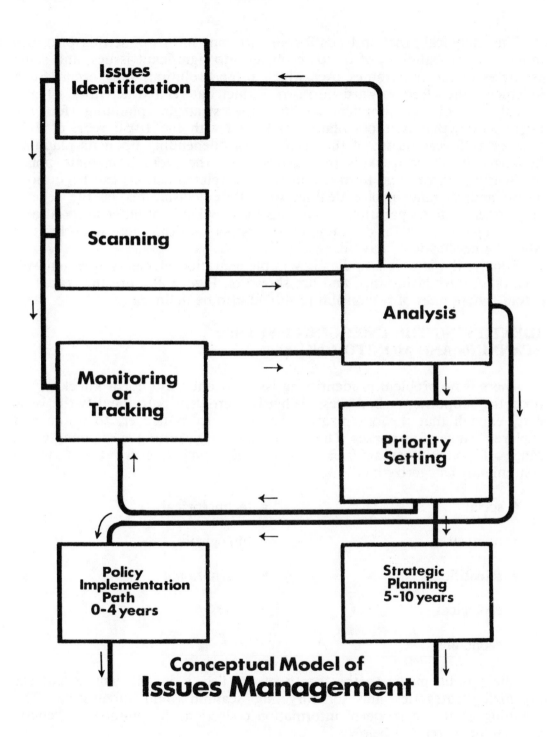

Figure 2-5. Conceptual Model of Issues Management
(Prepared by J.F. Coates, Inc.)

The analytical function leads forward to some means of setting priorities in terms of probabilities of trends evolving into significant issues, and some estimates of the timeframes over which those evolutions may occur. Such judgments then feed forward into two distinct but related activities. One is articulation of the implications for the strategic planning for the organization; that is, those plans which deal with the 10-50 year, or 7-40 year, or 5-25 year future of the organization, depending upon its planning horizon. The other track is into determining the more immediate policy implications, those areas in which more issues-related actions can begin now. Those actions may involve dealing with state legislatures or the federal government, site preparation, tooling up for new kinds of labor negotiations, or scanning markets for declining or new opportunities. There is no limit to what the implications may be.

Finally, the strategic and policy implementation elements interact with each other. Overlaying this, and not shown on Figure 2-5, are the corporate actors, whose lines of responsibility should also be defined.

IDENTIFYING THE EMERGING ISSUES: SCANNING AND MONITORING

There is no problem in identifying issues if one waits for a knock at the door, the subpoena, or bad press. What is a problem is to identify the issue early enough that the organization has room to maneuver, to frame and explore a range of responses. The key to that early warning is scanning a full range of potential areas from which issues may emerge. They can be conveniently categorized as:

- social
- political
- scientific
- ecological
- economic

- technological
- biological
- international
- others

There is no magic to the length of the list; it is only convenient for organizing categories and for targeting scanning and monitoring. The scanning itself is a mode of information collection. A common or generic approach is described below.

The objective of scanning is to look over the widest range of possible factors and to identify connections with the organization's function or business, and especially to identify the significant positive or negative effects that those factors could have on the organization and its activities. Monitoring is in practice closely related to scanning and often involves the same kind of activities. But it is more sharp in focus.

Monitoring is to watch, observe, check, and keep up with developments, usually in a well-defined area of interest for a very specific purpose. For example, scanning may identify the fact that Compound X, which is associated with one of an organization's products, is reported in an Eastern European medical journal to be associated with disease Y. Having picked that up in a scanning function, one may decide to monitor the scientific and biomedical literature with regard to both that material and that disease.

In general, the objectives in monitoring and tracking are to:

- Detect scientific, technical, economic, social, political, and ecological interactions and other events important to the company.

- Identify the nature and significance of such events.

- Define the potential threats or opportunities or major potential changes for the organization that are implied by those events.

- Inform management and staff.

- Begin or promote more detailed tracking of potential event sequences for threats and opportunities.

- Promote a future orientation.

- Provide continuous awareness and evaluation of trends to guide planning and action choices.

- Direct attention to a search for information on subjects not likely to otherwise be attended to.

- Inform management and staff of the need for anticipatory action; minimize reaction, stimulate proaction.

- Alert management and staff to trends which are converging, diverging, speeding up, slowing down, or interacting.

In accomplishing these goals, the primary resources available are:

- Internal staff specialists.

- The general pool of employees in the organization.

- An internal *ad hoc* team.

- The management.

- Support organizations such as trade associations and policy research firms.

- Information services.

- Government organizations and information services.

- *Ad hoc* arrangements such as consultants, specific commissioned studies, etc.

SOME APPROACHES TO ISSUES IDENTIFICATION

In this section, we define a series of increasingly sophisticated approaches now used by corporations and associations in the first stages of issues identification, i.e., scanning and tracking or monitoring.

- The most rudimentary and primitive system under the title of "Issues Identification" involves the assignment of a single individual to read a range of routine publications, usually some national newspapers, a few leading magazines, and some specialty publications. That material is then abstracted and some kind of internal newsletter produced. Often that same person will have responsibility for reviewing some public documents, Congressional hearings, and kindred material.

That process will often be complemented by a newsletter or trend information service. The internal newsletter, when prepared under such rudimentary conditions, is often distributed with the general expectation that it will prove useful.

- The next step up is to have that function assigned to a group of people, often in a public or consumer affairs office where, among them, they will spend a fraction of their time reading an agreed upon assortment of publications, extracting them, and coming together to share information and prepare material for the newsletter.

In both this and the above case, the specialist or specialists assigned the identification function generally welcome information from other people on the staff, and will often respond to requests or queries.

- The third step up represents a much more substantial and effective activity. It follows the pattern first laid down by the Trend Analysis Program (TAP) of the American Council of Life Insurance and since widely used in one or another embodiment in public and private organizations. That system involves the following elements:

  —A group we will nominally call the scanning office, or an individual we will call the chief scanner, recruits a group of volunteer scanners from around the company, at all levels and in all units. Working with these other people in the organization, the chief scanner will identify a list of target publications. These will include general publications, national newspapers and magazines, specialty publications, and professional and trade scientific publications. A minimum list might be 30; an expanded list might be 100.

  —Specific mutually agreed on reading assignments will be made with the members of the scanning pool. They will read these assigned publications, usually one or two, routinely, and fill out a scanning form (see Figure 2-6). That scanning form notes the publication or the source; attached is either the whole publication or a salient abstract, and the scanner's brief note of interpretation of significance to the company.

  —The chief scanner receives those materials on an ad lib basis and abstracts, collates, coordinates, and interprets them. In a fairly rudimentary system, the chief scanner issues abstracts based upon them in the form of a newsletter. Where some small number of topics have been identified as particularly important to the organization's future as potentially emerging issues, the chief scanner may set up a monitoring program to systematically examine sources of information about that topic. The chief scanner will alert all scanners to pay particular attention to the material relating to that topic being monitored. A sample monitoring form is shown in Figure 2-7.

- In the next step up in sophistication, still reflecting the TAP model, a steering committee or panel is formed which meets with the chief scanner to review, evaluate, and interpret the materials. They may also assign responsibility for digging deeper, building consensus, specific research, informing upper echelons of management, identifying R&D needs, or relating and tieing the issue into strategic considerations in terms of markets, research, personnel, planning, etc.

SAMPLE SCANNING REPORT FORMAT

Scanning   Date:

Topic Area:

Topic Title:

Source:

Description:

Potential Significance: Threat [   ]   Opportunity [   ]

Distribution: (code)

Action Recommended: (code)

Action Taken: (code)

Key Words for File & Access

Figure 2-6. Sample Scanning Report Format

Source: Prepared by Ralph Lenz of the University of Dayton for the
           Westinghouse Corporation.

SAMPLE MONITORING REPORT FORMAT

Subject: Date:

Lead Monitor:

Reporting Monitor:

Report Number:

Source:

Description:

Potential Significance: Threat [   ]   Opportunity [   ]

Distribution: (code)

Action Recommended: (code)

Action Taken: (code)

Key Words for File and Access

Figure 2-7. Sample Monitoring Report Format

Source: Prepared by Ralph Lenz of the University of Dayton for the Westinghouse Corporation.

By the time a system has reached this degree of sophistication there is almost surely some key word filing system, perhaps some computer assisted file with key word retrieval, and some more sophisticated internal communications system in which the material is presented in highly salient and focused ways. For example, in one large communications organization using approximately 100 scanners, there were three layers above the scanners. Scanners were situated all over the country and all over the company, feeding in their material to a layer of coordinators. The coordinators did a rough-cut evaluation of the information and fed it into the chief scanner's office. The scanner and the coordinators met periodically to review and evaluate this information and to select key issues. The key issues were each formulated into a brief issue paper, running six to ten pages. The issue papers then went forward to a senior advisory committee, where they were evaluated and decisions made as to their significance to the company. If appropriate, further evaluation and research were done, drawing on consultants or on internally or externally commissioned papers. If that material reinforced the significance of the emerging issue it was then brought to the next higher echelon.

That top echelon was a vice presidential level committee. The relative role of the chief scanner's office was muted in these higher echelon contacts to maximize credibility. Briefings were made by people with substantive organizational responsibilities closest to the echelon being briefed.

Two points should be noted. First, out of this process there may be incidental benefits not directly connected to the issues management, merely because people are meeting, talking, exchanging ideas, and getting to know each other in ways different from their usual hierarchical or bureaucratic context. Those exchanges always increase the likelihood of payoff.

Second, as embodied in the early TAP program, a pleasant amenity was often provided to the company-wide scanners: the chance to meet once a year and be exposed to a day of futures activity, with prominent futurists brought in for lectures, and discussion.

FURTHER DETAILS ON ISSUES IDENTIFICATION

There is no fixed way or even best practice for issues identification and the subsequent internal processing of the resulting material. An organization with a single product line, stable markets and supplies, and a relatively small number of sites of manufacturing, is in an entirely different position from a major conglomerate with fifty business units, scores of facilities, hundreds of marketing outlets, thousands of clients, and a variety of industrial, business, and consumer products. The ways in which issues are handled, therefore, vary widely. The use of external and internal support mechanisms also differs widely with the above variables and with the culture and customs of the organizations. However, three critical elements which enter into all successful issues management processes are education, analysis, and interpretation in terms of possible actions.

THE EDUCATION FUNCTION

Internal education and exchange of information are generally not enough. External resources often are called upon either passively or actively in educating senior managers and staff. These resources come in a variety of graded services:

- The most elementary service is the purchase of newsletters and proprietary information services.

- The next step up is the purchase of proprietary services which provide tailor-made consulting and interpretation. For example, one consulting organization provides external abstracts from publications it scans regularly plus specific ones processed for the client. The educational process is framed around quarterly meetings with client groups to discuss emerging trends, issues, and developments, and usually involves a further commitment to some individualized consulting days at the client's discretion.

- Another consultant service provides workbooks to be used in seminars with the client. The workbooks help to develop understanding and consensus on critical issues and actions.

ANALYTICAL AND INTERPRETATION FUNCTION

The interpretation function merges into the education function, and often the same people or some of the same people are involved in the two functions. The key analytical questions are:

- The timeframe of the evolving issue: is it imminent? Is it going to mature in the next three years or so? Will it be long in emerging, perhaps five or more years out?

- Is the situation likely to mature into a true issue?

- Assuming it matures into an issue, will it specifically affect this industry and this corporation? How might that effect occur?

There is no definitive way to answer these questions. Every significant process involves interaction, exchange of information, incremental development of further information, monitoring, targeted information collection and analysis, and often the use of relatively simple tools for clarification. These techniques are discussed in detail in chapter 3. It must be kept in mind that there is no magic here; there is no formula for addressing these critical questions. Process must dominate, and that process must be credible in terms of its actors, its inputs, its implications, and its interpretations.

ADDITIONAL CONSIDERATIONS IN ISSUES MANAGEMENT

Additional considerations on how any organization could begin to set up a useful issues identification and management system relate particularly to fitting issues management to the organization's customs, culture, and commitments.

Issues management systems in industry and trade associations tend to settle into one of three organizational locations: public relations, policy analysis, or strategic planning. To commit solely to any of these three locations is probably a mistake. A comprehensive program must deal with both long-term implications for the organization (five, ten, or more years in the future), and with the intermediate implications three to five years ahead, and also relate to the more immediate pressing issues. The defining theme is the long-term interests of the corporation, not short-term fire fighting.

Those already sold on the values of issues management may be prepared to go immediately to a relatively extensive and costly arrangement. Others may feel that an incremental approach, starting modestly and learning by doing, is more appropriate. Either approach can work: a relatively low cost system, or a higher cost and more complex alternative. But consensus in the field is that one should not jump into issues identification and management as a full-blown technical initiative. Substantial work must go into nurturing the development of a system that fits the organization.

Consequently, a first move into issues identification and management should be a low cost, highly flexible system started as a trial, evaluation, and learning experience with the anticipation that the successful elements will be built upon, and the less successful elements modified or dropped. With increased sophistication and experience, more expensive, comprehensive, or complex elements may be added to the functioning system. Put briefly, high cost versus low cost is a false dichotomy. With a firm commitment, the early effort should be relatively bounded, but premised on the expectation that with experience the process will be augmented and expanded as appropriate.

It is not necessary to have a huge budget or staff. One experienced person, preferably someone who understands the structure of the industry, full-time, and given a secretary, a budget of $40,000 - $50,000 per year (including subscriptions), and $10,000 - $15,000 for travel—he has to get out and talk to people—would be a good beginning. He can use some outside services, but he also needs to tap the expertise within the company and to get offices to assign a person to monitor for the scanning process.

Before considering further details of any suggested systems for issues management, the kernels of advice on starting an issues management program gleaned from our interviews are noted.

ADVICE ON GETTING STARTED

In many of the interviews with corporate issues managers, consultants, and people providing backup services, we asked for their two or three statements of best advice to an individual or an organization starting an issues identification and management program.

Some of the following points are almost direct quotes; others are paraphrases or digests. Since many of them have a pungency that could be embarrassing, we have eliminated all attribution.

1. As an analyst, be a resource. Do not try to be an issues manager. Do not try to run the show. Be a backstop and backup for those who have organizational responsibility. Neither seek nor accept issues management if your role is issues analysis.

2. Be positive, but do not be Pollyannish. The responsibility of an analyst sometimes requires dark warnings of undesirable developments.

3. If you can't sell it to senior managers, forget it.

4. Once you are setup, go to the grass roots in the organization, reach down into the organization. As you identify your issues, set priorities among them. Set up strategies based on those priorities. Provide feedback.

5. Don't preempt the functions or activities of others; be a helpmate; this cuts jealousy and conflict.

6. Issues identification, etc., is primarily a service and support function.

7. Don't act as if you have or pretend to have a fundamental lock on appropriate knowledge.

8. Do what fits; that is, what fits the company's culture, its ethos, its organizational structure.

9. Get the management of an issue into that part of the company where it fits. For example, an environmental issue should be handled in that part of the company that is connected with the environmental concern.

10. There must be some corporate outreach in order to lift horizons; public affairs tend to focus on the short range. Lifting horizons can be accomplished in part by specially commissioned studies or other kinds of services.

11. The key is not identifying and describing issues; the key lies in how one makes them part of the running of the business.

12. In many situations, you will need to build your team around two people; the first is someone who understands the company—an insider who will have good access into internal networks and effective internal communication. The complementary person should have solid experience in trend analysis.

13. It takes two to four years for an issue to pass through the company, from early identification to maturation and effective handling. Issues management staffing should be planned with that in mind.

14. Your team should be interdisciplinary, including operational people; in order to get a full treatment of the issue in terms of the who, the when, the where it should be handled, and the how it should be handled.

15. Do a good job building a consensus on expectations about what the issues management process will yield. Note that half of the benefits will be gravy; that is, not part of the original expectations.

16. People doing an analysis should be insightful and skilled and articulate in delivering information.

17. Close attention should be given to what to look at, in terms of survival value of the company and the ability to grab the attention of the senior managers.

18. Approach an issue as if you come from another planet, as if you have no preconceptions or biases, from an almost childish point of view. Put things together in your mind in different ways. Ask, how do these pieces fit together? Create alternate scenarios in your mind.

19. Issues analysis is critical to management, but remember it is a service to management and a mechanism by which management moves forward.

20. Decide either you want the credit for what you do or you want something to happen; you cannot have both.

21. Take the team or task force approach. Drawing on different areas, let them decide on an effective approach for the group. Spread the responsibility around and use the task force to develop an educational program spreading responsibility further. (But don't call it educational.) Most managers will not be able to deal with the kind qualitative information usually produced, and the techniques look too social science for this.

22. Network!

23. Don't use consultants. Mostly corporations do not know how to use them. Okay if you want a general information dump—but corporations also need to know how to sort the useful information out and this is not possible unless you have a long-term relationship with the consultants and they really know your business.

24. Very little happens which is not embodied in some way in state or local legislation (bills) first, usually introduced by some zealous legislator. Pay attention to these bills, study the concepts behind them, and track the issue from the moment when it crosses the magic threshold, i.e., the committee chairman, or a more powerful legislator takes action.

25. Don't set up an IM program unless you have the Chairman's support.

26. Know your company very well, its strengths and weaknesses.

27. Establish and manage a finite number of major issues.

28. Find out what your organizational needs are.

29. Understand how to communicate issues management through your style of corporation; for example, is it centralized or decentralized?

30. Establish a comfortable level of manpower to satisfy the needs of IM in the organization.

31. Start slowly in order to overcome an important philosophical barrier; that is, the demand for prediction, for statements of what issues will occur. It is necessary to educate the group as to what issues are, what strategic planning is, the relationship of issues to strategic planning, and what to expect from issues management. If you go too fast, and get out ahead of the group, you will be discredited.

32. There are five keys:

    —Understand what strategy means.

    —Manage issues; to do that one needs a business intelligence system, teamwork, and line responsibilities.

    —Manage telematics. Learn about the new technologies of telecommunications and computers and what they mean to you.

    —Create a strategic organization; make clear the lines of responsibility for study and management of issues; have a flat, broad, lean structure; have participatory strategic management circles.

    —Learn to manage thinking. Most organizations simply do not know how to think, how to encourage it. Thinking is an art which can be taught and must be practiced.

33. House issues identification in strategic planning, and hire people who can deal with the long-term. I have never seen a true issues identification program in a public affairs department.

34. The purpose of an IM program is the long-term survival and benefit to the company. In contrast, often people who say they want an IM program simply want a government relations program to manage legislative activity. This is a good governmental affairs job but it is not issue identification.

35. Senior management has to want this process, has to understand it, has to accept what it throws up, and exercise their prerogatives of policy analysis and decision-making.

36. Success is hard to measure because issues management is a process; however, it is generally understood when an outcome is acceptable to a company.

37. Our most valuable area of work is in informed judgment. Since you can never get enough information, you are forced to expert opinion.

38. Only take the top big issues up to the most senior management—four or five at the most. A hundred or two hundred issues are too many, and must be left at the lower management or staff operating levels.

AN ALTERNATIVE POINT OF VIEW

The published literature on issues management is strongly positive about issues management, and relatively uncritical. It presents a strong case that issues management is timely, along with many specific accounts of how it is done, and the value of various approaches, techniques, and strategies. The overwhelming sense of the literature is that issues management is useful, effective, and doable.

In sharp contrast, the interviews with practitioners brought to the surface a minority, but substantial, counteropinion. These negative conclusions, we emphasize were a minority opinion, but they were expressed often enough by experienced practitioners that the counteropinion requires recognition and acknowledgment.

There is strong consensus that issues management should be integrated into the company's line activities, and should not be merely a centralized or public affairs staff function. Responsibility should lie with those with the greatest stake in implementation. The counteropinion went well beyond this to say that there should be no formal programs. Decentralization and flexibility should dominate all other factors in the management approach to emerging issues.

Going along with this was a common thread that there should be no formal function other than an educational one to increase awareness of issues and the possibility of issues management. This counter position frames itself around a crucial observation: linking awareness of the issue to decision-making is absolutely necessary. Any formalism tends to be a barrier to that linkage.

There was also a strong expression of negative opinion toward issues managers. People associated with public affairs functions, as one analyst put it, are quite good at dealing with external actors, but generally fall short internally in dealing with operating divisions. Issues managers were seen, in the counteropinion, to be dealing with the wrong issues and to be the wrong messengers.

We believe these counter views represent a reaction to bad experience or are perhaps over-stated versions of solid, hard earned lessons. But the reader should know about them.

LOCATING ISSUES IDENTIFICATION AND MANAGEMENT IN THE ORGANIZATION

The apparent implicit assumption in the material presented so far is that issues management should be approached as an organization-wide activity, enjoying the endorsement and approval if not the active, aggressive participation of senior management. An important question arises: is it practical to start an issues identification and management system without that high level, active support?

The answer, of course, is "yes." Most issues identification activities have evolved out of working units of an organization, often those concerned with public affairs. In some cases the issues management activity has tended to remain there formally while dealing with higher and higher levels of management. In other organizations the function has been moved out of the sub-unit and into the top executive suite.

One particularly interesting example of beginning at a lower level or with a specific function within the organization is reflected in the formation of an *ad hoc* consortium called the Environmental Scanning Association, representing the human resources concerns of eighteen major American corporations. The active members of the association are the human resources managers in these major corporations. They have found the association along their special interests fruitful, and have even commissioned papers and studies in support of their collective concern.

It should be noted, however, that one of the characteristics of the human resources area is that it affects many aspects of the organization's activities and in turn is affected by a large number of external factors such as workforce demographics, economic conditions, legal and regulatory developments, technological change, social change, international affairs, and scores of other areas. Therefore, it is a microcosm of the forces, factors, and issues affecting the corporation at large.

3

METHODS AND TECHNIQUES OF ISSUES MANAGEMENT

INTRODUCTION

The methods and techniques applicable to issues management are like the brick, stone, and mortar in constructing a building. They are essential, but they cannot guarantee a successful design. To bridge the gap between technique in the narrow sense and successful design of an issues management program, we address in this chapter process aspects of issues management, such as networking and executive juries. The techniques are not handled in a uniform way, since that would to some degree falsify understanding of some of the methods.

The techniques are discussed below, in order:

- networking
- precursor analysis, bellwethers
- media analysis (column inch counting)
- polls and surveys
- juries of executive opinion
- expert panels
- scanning and monitoring
- content analysis
- legislative tracking
- Delphi
- conversational Delphi
- consensor

- cross impact analysis
- decision support systems
- computer assisted techniques
- small group process
- scenario building
- trend extrapolation
- technological forecasting
- decision analysis
- factor analysis
- sensitivity analysis
- trigger event identification
- key player analysis
- correlation/regression

A general outline of factors for evaluating these techniques follows. The use of the evaluation factors is implicit in many of the technique descriptions. Figure 3-1 summarizes the status of each of the techniques by these evaluation factors.

For each technique there is an introductory description and, in most cases, a discussion of time and cost and a summary. For some techniques there is an expanded discussion of uses or additional comments, as appropriate.

EVALUATION FACTORS	Relevance to IM	Importance to IM	Labor Cost	Expertise to Use	Services Available	Use in Startup	Use in Steady State	Transfer-ability to New Users	Understand-able to Management	Do-able by Management	Validity
TECHNIQUES											
Networking	H	H	H	L	S	M	H	L	H	M	H
Precursor Events, Bellwethers	M	M	H	H	S	L	M	M	M	L	L–H
Media Analysis, (Col. Inch Counting)	M	M	M	H	F	L	M	H	M	L	L–H
Polls/Surveys	M	M	H	H	M	L	M	H	M	L	L–H
Executive Jury	H	H	L	L	NA	H	H	H	H	H	L–H
Expert Panel	M	H	H	H	M	L	L	M	H	H	L–H
Scanning & Monitoring	H	H	M–H	M	S	H	H	H	M	L	M–H
Content Analysis	M	M	H	M	F	L	M	L	L	L	M–H
Legislative Tracking	H	M	H	M	S	L	H	L	M	L	M–H
Delphi	L	L	M	H	M	L	L	L	L	L	L–M
Conversational Delphi	H	M	M	H	S	L	L	L	H	L	H
Consensor	M	L	L	L	NA	L	L	H	M–H	H	H
Cross-Impact	H	M	L–H	H	S	M	M	M	M–H	M	M–H
Decision Support Systems	H	M	M	L–M	F	L	M	M	M–H	M	M–H
Computer Assisted Techniques	H	M	M–H	M	M	L	H	L	L–M	L	M–H
Small Group Process	H	H	L	H	M	H	H	L	H	H	M–H
Scenario Building	M	M	H	M	M	L	M	L	L–H	L	L–H
Trend Extrapolation	M	H	H	H	S	M	H	L	L–H	L	L–H
Technological Forecasting	L	L	H	H	S	L	L	L	L–H	L	L–H
Decision Analysis	L	L	–	H	F	NA	NA	L	L	L	L–H
Factor Analysis	L	L	–	H	M	NA	NA	L	L	L	M–H
Sensitivity Analysis	L	L	–	H	M	NA	NA	L	L	L	M–H
Trigger Event Identification	M	M	–	H	F	L	M	L	L–M	L	L–H
Key Player Analysis	M	M	M	H	F	H	H	L	M–H	M	M–H
Correlation/ Regression	L	L	–	H	M	NA	NA	L	L	L	L–H

CODE:
H — High
M — Medium
L — Low, Long
NA — No Application
UNK — Unknown

0–2 (years) Near term
2–5 (years) Mid-term
5–50 (years) Long-term

S — Some, Short
M — Many
F — Few

Figure 3-1. Summary Matrix: Issues Management Techniques and Evaluation Factors

Source: J.F. Coates, Inc.

EVALUATION FACTORS	Scope of Use in Industry	Startup Time	Database Requirements	Inter-Personal Skills Reqd.	Usable in Advisory Framework	Understand-able to Advisors	Time Horizon	Capital Cost	Application to Strategic Planning	Use of Computers
TECHNIQUES										
Networking	M	L	L	H	H	H	0–5+	L	M	L
Precursor Events, Bellwethers	M	L	H	L	M	M	0–5+	L	M–H	M
Media Analysis, (Col. Inch Counting)	M	S	M	L	M	M	0–2	L	L–M	H
Polls/Surveys	M	S	M	L	M	M	0–2	L	L–H	H
Executive Jury	M	S	L	H	H	H	0–5+	L	L–H	L
Expert Panel	S	S	L	H	H	H	0–5+	L	L–H	L
Scanning & Monitoring	S	S	M	M	M	M	0–5+	L	L–H	M–H
Content Analysis	F	L	M	L	L	L	0–5+	L	L–H	H
Legislative Tracking	M	L	H	L	L	M	0–5+	L	L–H	M–H
Delphi	F	S	L	L	H	M	0–5+	L	M–H	M–H
Conversational Delphi	F	S	L	H	H	H	0–5+	L	M–H	L
Consensor	F	S	L	H	H	H	0–5+	L	L–H	H
Cross-Impact	F	S	L–H	H	L	L	0–5+	L	M–H	L–H
Decision Support Systems	F	L	M–H	L	L	M	0–5+	M	L–H	H
Computer Assisted Techniques	M	L	M–H	L	M	M	0–5+	M–H	L–H	H
Small Group Process	M	S	L	H	H	H	0–5+	L	L–H	L–M
Scenario Building	S	L	M–H	H	L–M	M	0–5+	L–H	M–H	L–H
Trend Extrapolation	M	L	M–H	M	L	M	0–5+	L	M–H	M–H
Technological Forecasting	M	L	M–H	L	L	M	0–5+	L	M–H	M–H
Decision Analysis	UNK	UNK	UNK	L	NA	M	0–5+	L	M–H	H
Factor Analysis	UNK	UNK	UNK	L	NA	M	UNK	L	M–H	H
Sensitivity Analysis	UNK	UNK	UNK	L	NA	M	UNK	L	M–H	H
Trigger Event Identification	UNK	UNK	UNK	M	M	L	0–5+	L	L	L
Key Player Analysis	UNK	UNK	UNK	M	M	L	0–5+	L	L–M	L
Correlation/Regression	UNK	UNK	UNK	L	L	M	UNK	L	M–H	HG

CODE:
H — High
M — Medium
L — Low, Long
NA — No Application
UNK — Unknown

0–2 (years) — Near term
2–5 (years) — Mid-term
5–50 (years) — Long-term

S — Some, Short
M — Many
F — Few

Figure 3-1 (cont.)

Evaluation Factors

Since issues management is a comprehensive process involving a wide range of users or issues disparate in time, content, and importance, it is difficult to assign an unequivocal evaluation to many of the techniques that have been used or could be applied to issues management. Figure 3-1 summarizes the status of each of the techniques in terms of twenty considerations. Those evaluations are presented in qualitative rather than quantitative terms using such phrases as "high," "medium," "low," "some," "short," "many," and "few." The qualitative evaluations avoid misleading the reader and would-be user by over-quantification or over-specification.

The twenty evaluation factors are:

- Relevance to issues management.

- Importance to issues management.

- Labor costs.

- The expertise needed to use the technique.

- The availability of external support services, consulting assistance, etc.

- The applicability to the startup of an issues management program.

- Use in a mature or well established program.

- Transferability to other users, that is, the technique lends itself to ready adoption and transfer from one person to another.

- Understandable to management.

  —A technique, if it is to affect an organization's operation, must be either understandable by the management, which enhances its credibility, or must be implicitly accepted by them on the basis of confidence in the staff. The more understandable the techniques leading to issues identification and the evolution of action options, the more likely that technique and its findings are to be credible.

- Doability by management.

  —Since senior management commitment, if not involvement, in issues management is generally seen as an indispensable feature of a program, techniques which can be used with senior managers to enhance their understanding of an issue can be valuable.

- Scope of use in industry.

   —Refers to the experience with a tool across all business and industrial users. Our designation of "some," "few," and "many" is highly judgmental and subject to revision. The techniques used by specific firms are generally not well known nor easily determined. The number of interviews conducted in this project is small compared to the universe of possible users.

- Startup time.

   —Time is relative to other techniques and relative to the needs of the organization. Some startup times are long because of the need to acquire equipment and lay it in place, as with the decision support system. Others are long because they require an accretion of material or a great deal of experience. Some techniques, on the other hand, can be used immediately.

- Database requirements.

   —This factor is important to both startup and to the overall financial commitments to the process. Fortunately, many of the most applicable techniques have small database requirements and can often be handled on an *ad hoc* basis permitting relatively ready startup.

- Interpersonal skills required.

   —This is an extremely important criterion, since the issues management crew must deal with senior managers and with their colleagues throughout the company.

- Usable in an advisory framework.

   —Recognizing the importance but the severe limitations on advisory mechanisms, the selection of some technique for application by those groups is important in an organization with high dependence on membership participation or on large or numerous advisory bodies.

- Understandability to advisors.

  —Again, the same contrast is made as with managers, understandable and applicable are important but distinctly different criteria. In many cases, one would want in an organization driven by advisory apparatuses to be sure that the techniques were at a minimum understandable by the advisory mechanisms as an important credibility criterion.

- Time horizon.

  —Refers to the applicability of the technique to the emerging time of issue. For example, Column Inch Counting is effectively a relatively immediate technique applicable to current or rapidly emerging issues. On the other hand, technological forecasting is much more open ended and can deal with issues from the immediate to the quite long-term.

- Capital costs.

  —Capital costs of almost all the techniques are low, except for those which require computer assistance or a large data base.

- Application to strategic planning.

  —The issues identified in programs under discussion may be relatively short or long-term in their implications and would therefore have to integrate with different functioning elements of the organization. Most of the techniques are applicable to a medium or high degree to strategic planning.

- Use of computers.

  —Virtually none of the techniques require computational assistance. On the other hand, information support systems, modern office automation technology, data processing and display tools have some established and potential application to almost every technique. And in almost all cases there is a body of applicable literature, technology, support services, and software packages. The general sense of the experience is that early dependence on computer assisted techniques is almost surely a misstep if the application of computer technology in any way becomes a substitute for the interactive, small group, human process and networking side of an issues management program.

Some Additional Considerations

Several evaluation factors that immediately jump to mind as important with regard to methods and techniques present substantial difficulties and are not used as evaluation factors. The most important of these are validity and quantification.

- *Validity* is taken to mean how good the track record of the technique is in identifying, defining, and shaping response, and how effective the resultant response is in coping with the emerging situation. Little can be said of any significance about the validity of any of these techniques. The over emphasis on validity suggests an attempt to push what is an art form into a disciplinary, scientific model.

Many of the issues managers interviewed made it clear that they had tried many of the techniques discussed in this section. The general feeling is that the selection of techniques depends mostly on fitting the organization's structure and management style. Some people felt strongly that quantitative techniques were of very limited value to them; others felt that computer assisted techniques were extremely valuable in special cases. Virtually everyone emphasized process, interaction, and networking as the dominant features of an effective system.

Successful cases of issues identification and management involve a relatively long-time, multi-step, multi-tier management system. No single technique in that complex process would stand out as the key tool. Consequently, the attempt to attribute validity to the processes is more misleading than enlightening.

- *Quantification* is a second, generally desirable criterion in terms of both a scientific model and an organizational model, since numbers are the common coinage in both areas. Unfortunately, except as noted in column inch counting, polls, and surveys, there are few applications for objective numbers. Many of the techniques use subjective numbers, as in cross impact and scenario development. Again, quantification as a goal or a technique is off center in issues management. Some organizations in sorting out their priorities may very well use some kind of cost benefit or cost effectiveness criterion in terms of the size of the operation affected, the percent of the business influenced, and the possible significance of cost to the company. On the other hand, even these cost criteria are not always applicable, since some organizations find issues which are relatively low cost, such as some labor relations or consumer issues, to be extremely important. Consequently, in the discussions below the quantifications are only touched upon and not made central to the presentation.

Figure 3-1 summarizes the status of each of the techniques by the evaluation factors discussed above. The reader may wish to look at that exhibit before turning to the discussion of the techniques.

THE TECHNIQUES

Technique: Networking

There is strong consensus among successful practitioners of issues management that networks of relationships, inside and outside the company, are critical to:

- Identifying issues.

- Checking the validity of one's concerns and judgments.

- Identifying the wider range of interested parties and strategies for response.

- The exchange of professional information about methods, techniques, substance, and process.

There is no rule or formula for setting up a network or joining a network. The following illustrates some ways in which networks can be engaged:

- Issues managers from ten diverse companies, not in the same industrial sector, meet frequently, but not regularly.

- Some commercial services supporting issues management bring their clients together for periodic meetings to discuss issues and their interpretation. For example, it is characteristic of the STEP Program of Weiner Edrich Brown, Inc.

- *Ad hoc* arrangements provide an opportunity to network; for example, United Way has a blue ribbon advisory board of futurists, planners, and issues managers. Obviously, their getting together to assist United Way widens their own networks.

- Attendance at Association meetings, such as the twice yearly meetings of the Issues Management Association, puts one in contact with practitioners, consultants, academics, etc. The twice yearly meetings of the Public Affairs Council have been held since 1977. The Spring meeting on fundamentals is an introduction or brushup. The meeting later in the year is a more advanced engagement of issues.

- An interesting variation on networking was that tried by a major retailer operating on the assumption that 90% of the benefit of dealing with a consultant comes in the first 10% of the expenditures. He bought a small block of time from each of a large number of futures consulting firms. Their output formed a useful first order analysis of a complex problem.

- The Trend Analysis Program of the American Council of Life Insurance at one time provided an annual meeting for its scanners. It drew together a substantial number of people from company members of the Council.

Internal networking in a corporation is crucial to the success of any issues management program. The issues manager is sure to fail if he or she assumes that the function is primarily to analyze written material, present written digests, and distribute them to staff and management. We have been unable to identify any successful program operating on that basis.

An issues management program fitting the culture, goals, objectives, internal power structure, and ambience of the specific company management implies that the issue manager has a great deal of face-to-face contact with his full range of internal constituents. As one analyst put it, the substantive work only comprises about 20% of the activities of the person involved in issues management. The rest of the time and effort is taken up with the organization, orchestration, packaging, delivery of information, and taking care of all the necessary internal matters to make such a program effective.

Within a trade association operating an effective issues management program, networking is a core activity in serving the client membership. That networking would include contacts in the member companies, meetings, training programs, analysis and evaluation sessions, information transfer, interpretation, and *ad hoc* services to the clients. Networking, of course, at the trade association level, external to the association and to those other than members of the association would be accomplished by the same techniques described for the corporate issues manager. It is useful to network to other trade associations, since there are some specific lessons to be learned in servicing a membership organization not generally important inside a company.

Time. Networking will settle down to some average factor in the total allocation of time. One can anticipate that networking could be relatively a higher proportion of the activities during startup when one is collecting lessons learned, establishing first networks, and building a constituency.

Cost. Costs will vary, depending upon the extent to which one uses commercial services, whose primary values will to some extent lie in other directions, namely, the formal information they provide. Most of the cost of networking will be as overhead, since it will not generally be directly chargeable to a particular project, task, or effort. In other words, networking is part of being an effective professional worker. Since networking involves contacts outside as well as within the organization, one can anticipate substantial travel costs, telephone bills, and other incidental costs associated with outreach to those outside the organization.

Summary. The overwhelming value of networking, both internal and external to the organization, would be difficult to exaggerate. Effective networking goes beyond the immediate company or organizational framework and outside one's sector to draw upon a wide range of skill, talent, perspective, and to learn about alternative methods and techniques and to confirm or disconfirm one's judgments about emerging issues.

Technique: Precursor Analysis - Bellwether Jurisdictions

Precursor analysis is one of the oldest techniques of formal futures studies. Condorcet, the first of the great modern futurists who flourished at the period of the French Revolution, observed that what the wealthy eat, drink, and do today become the food, recreation, and pastimes of the less well-to-do tomorrow. He discovered trickle down.

In the contemporary era it is widely recognized that events which occur in Sweden and the other Scandinavian countries often occur later in the United States. It is widely believed that what goes on in California often, if not always, becomes the pattern in the rest of the nation. These informal and perhaps overgeneralized observations have become the contemporary basis for precursor analysis.

Precursor analysis today consists of some mixture of trend correlation and argument by analogy. In one systematic study of Sweden as a precursor country, it was found that in such major areas as auto safety, environmental issues, and the social control of alcoholism, the overwhelming majority of social and policy events occurred in Sweden before they occurred in the United States. According to Graham Molitor, one of the leading exponents of precursor analysis, "the lead/lag time between Western Europe and the United States is 22 years in social policy, 6 to 8 years in consumer policy, and 2 to 4 years in environmental policy." Therefore, studying events occurring in precursor nations, such as England, France, and Sweden, aids in predicting which events may occur when in the United States. Using European precursor events, Molitor cites the case of one food company that tracked a food coloring issue in Europe and anticipated that it would become an issue in the United States. Meanwhile, the company worked out its solution in the laboratory, and even had press releases ready to go, when several years later the issue did come to a head in the United States.

By no means are there only precursor nations. There are precursor states and local governments, and other jurisdictions.

The most common form of precursor analysis now widely practiced is in the search for the bellwether states.

The leading exponent of precursor analysis in the form of bellwether state concepts is the Naisbitt Group. Naisbitt argues that most of the social inventions in America occur in just five states, California, Florida, Washington, Colorado, and Connecticut. The concept is brought to practical application in that organization's publication, *The Bellwether Report*, a monthly regionally targeted analysis, which focuses on states where most social invention first occurs. It carries a $357 annual fee.

Our interviews with practical issues managers took a more textured and pointed analysis, basically leading to the conclusion that there are no universal bellwether states. On particular issues, some states generally seem to be in the lead of the rest of the nation. For example, Oregon seems to be good on environmental matters, but not particularly a precursor on taxes. Florida seems to be good on privacy and on health issues, and Tennessee seems to be a good bellwether in pharmaceuticals. It is rather obvious that the search should be for the earliest bellwether states. The bellwether concept smoothly flows into a form of precursor analysis, in which the mere tallying of the number of instances of a policy issue being discussed in a state legislature and the number of bills coming forward identify a strong trend.

In terms of the family of precursor analysis techniques, Figure 2-3 perhaps is the most comprehensive display of the kinds of precursor events, ranging from scientific discoveries to full and continual appearance in the national press.

If one chose to monitor international precursor nations, the obvious choice of a half dozen or more to monitor would include Sweden, Norway, Denmark, The Netherlands, Switzerland, West Germany, Great Britain, the United States, Canada, Australia, and Japan. It is widely agreed that for many international trends the U.S. is the precursor country.

In terms of domestic precursor or bellwether jurisdictions at the local government level, New York City and State, Boston, Massachusetts, California, and New Jersey, are leaders. At the county level, Dade County, Florida, is a relatively new bellwether. Laggards in almost all regards are Mississippi, Alabama, and South Dakota.

There are many kinds of support services available at the state and local government level, but particularly at the state level.

State governments themselves face much the same range of problems that a corporation does in keeping abreast of developments in other states. A new and somewhat grandiose plan is afoot out of the Council of State Planning Agencies to work with people out of the Governors' offices to form a nationwide network on emerging issues identification and policy generation.

Of more direct service to the corporation is *State Policy*, a clearinghouse publication on state governmental affairs for professionals published by the National Center for Legislative Research.

Custom services are available from organizations such as State and Federal Associates, Washington, D.C. That organization has a slightly different twist to the state level argument, namely, that what is neglected at the federal level will be addressed at the state level. Their expertise is on the procedural side of working at either the legislative or executive side of state activities. Their service is to help a client understand the full panoply of actors, issues, and procedures connected with what they might do. So, for example, on a bank acquisition, they might help the client understand what the short-term and long-term practicalities and limitations are on an acquisition. For a drug manufacturer whose product is making a transition from prescription to over the counter, they might work the question of how to get it accepted by Medicare in a particular state.

Time. Precursor or bellwether analysis is labor intensive. It depends upon the accumulation of a substantial body of experience, the development of skills and interpretation, and time to test and evaluate one's conclusions against implications and outcomes. Consequently, the technique in terms of time is not one to be undertaken lightly, early, or in some initial phase of startup as an internal activity. However, much of the early learning and much of the continuing labor can be managed through the purchase of the numerous services noted. Services, however, at best will only augment the necessary internal activities and commitment to time.

Cost. Because of the nature of the time commitment and labor intensivity, precursor and bellwether analysis is a relatively costly process and should not be entered into lightly. One can, of course, as mentioned, purchase services, the cost of some of which have been indicated. But basically the primary cost will be internal labor costs for data collection, analysis, and interpretation.

Summary. Bellwether and precursor analysis is an important technique, widely employed with different levels of intensity and scope by many organizations. It is extremely well suited to the electric utility industry, as a nationwide but highly distributed industry with strong impacts from state and local government and community action groups. The transferability of lessons from bellwether concepts is, therefore, likely to be quite high. Furthermore, from the science and technology point of view, the application of a technology overseas as well as in the United States also lends itself to bellwether applications.

Technique: Media Analysis (Column Inch Counting)

The media are a key source of virtually every kind of information of concern to the issues manager. This particular section, based on in-depth discussions with the publisher of *Issues Management Letter*, reports on one form of quantification of the media content.

That *Letter* is a biweekly report of percent of media space occupied by ten top issues, as reported on three TV networks, five major newspapers, and three national news magazines. The numbers are collated, manipulated, and presented in a variety of indices and formats. (See Figure 3-2.)

This particular technique is based upon the assumption that the media represent a "national voice" because of their national coverage, their close linkages to each other, linkages across media, the high level of communication among newsmen, the fact that the United States is a continental nation, and the media give relatively little attention to international and foreign news. This leads to the working assumption that it makes sense in terms of content analysis to identify the message that national voice is delivering.

The technique described below involves the identification and analysis of specific content messages in the national press, national news magazines, and national television, and emphasizes the importance of a message being delivered by the media. It contrasts with other content analysis techniques which use the media as a source of information about individual events, which are, in turn, analyzed, codified, collated, and reported.

The quantification of news content is essential to organizing and processing data, to identifying trends, and for comparability of information. The net effect of the quantification is a continuing measure of public exposure to issues in the national media.

Preparation of the *Issues Management Letter* involves a framework of 400 pre-selected issues which are used as bins into which the content of the newspaper are sorted. The reader, over a period of one to one-and-a-half hours, analyzes the content of one newspaper in terms of these 400 categories. A basic, empirically grounded assumption is that there is a fixed "news hole," that is, a fixed amount of news reported on the average by the press. This news hole turns out to be surprisingly stable and varies only slightly from major paper to major paper. The count, therefore, results in a percent of the news reporting on a particular issue. The material is directly entered into a computer. It should be noted that stories from the national press, from the point of view of newspaper technique, tend to be good stories in that they limit themselves to a single theme. Every two weeks, the ten issues representing the bulk of the coverage are selected out for reporting. A similar technique applies to the three national news magazines.

5/21 — 6/3/84

ISSUES	PERSIAN GULF	MONEY WORRIES	HEALTH	FAIRNESS	CORP. GOVERNANCE	ADMINISTRATION, CRIT.	ANTITRUST	DRUG/ALCOHOL ABUSE	*WOMEN	TRADE	AUDIENCE
ABC	39	2	13	2	8	6	1	6	1	2	13.5 mill.*
CBS	32	3	17	4	3	3	1	8	3	1	16.2' '
NBC	28	1	8	10	3	6	--	--	2	3	13.6' '
TOTAL (minutes)	99	6	38	16	14	15	2	14	6	6	Daily avg. as of 4/1/84
Chicago Trib.	736	1119	181	537	249	92	617	76	300	209	.79 mill.**
L.A. Times	774	633	142	524	227	88	460	62	171	392	1.08' '
N.Y Times	1148	1209	297	470	428	400	673	94	130	377	.96' '
Wall St. J.	225	1394	128	170	492	112	749	--	53	413	1.93' '
Wash. Post	1095	1240	285	738	167	794	506	41	155	210	.75' '
TOTAL (column inches)	3978	5595	1033	2439	1563	1486	3005	273	809	1601	---------------
Newsweek	120	124	35	94	70	22	10	240	90	20	3.0' '
Time	90	46	290	206	30	43	86	6	200	46	4.5' '
U.S. News	160	935	90	108	12	28	--	9	12	76	2.1' '
TOTAL (column inches)	370	1105	415	408	112	93	96	255	302	142	Daily avg. as of 1/18/84
EXPOSURE INDEX	10.4	7.7	4.7	3.9	2.2	2.2	2.2	2.0	1.9	1.8	---------------
5/20/84	3.3	7.7	1.4	4.2	2.5	1.4	1.4	0.2	1.9	1.3	---------------
5/6/84	0.6	3.3	3.0	1.9	1.7	1.6	2.3	0.2	0.1	2.1	------------

*Women as a subset of Fairness

INDEX NUMBERS USED IN THE CHART ABOVE AND THROUGHOUT THE TEXT IN PARENTHESES ( ) REPRESENT THE PERCENTAGE OF NATIONAL NEWS CAPACITY GIVEN TO AN ISSUE IN THE PREVIOUS TWO WEEKS. We use the eleven media shown above as proxies for all national media in making this analysis. Percentages of total news space devoted to each issue are calculated for each medium. Results are totalled by category and weighted in accordance with survey data on how Americans with college-entry level education seek information on public issues. The index draws on the work of Dr. Robert T. Bower of the Bureau of Social Sciences Research in Washington, D.C. His surveys show this group draws its information in the following ratios: TV—6; Newspapers—4; Magazines—3. Note: TV minutes are based on 1/2-hour nightly news programs for each network. We have found by examination for this to be fully representative of networks' news load.

Figure 3-2. Public Exposure: Top Ten Issues in the National Media

The TV coverage presents a somewhat different situation. No item is taken into account which occupies less than ten seconds. The TV programs are taped as backup; the operating assumption is that the East Coast news represents the national perspective, although there might be variations if one took a West Coast news source.

Time and Labor. The preparation of the analyses as described above occupies the equivalent of four full-time professionals, resulting in the direct readout of the percentages and critical interpretations of the material.

One estimate is that it would take six months of close supervision to train someone to do the job.

We have been unable to find any information on the value of this service from the point of view of users or subscribers, although the publisher claims that the technique has been successful in a number of areas, such as predicting the winners of the Presidential primaries in each state (with the possible exception of the State of California.)

Cost. As with many related services, this one can be extended to regional press, state level or sectorial press, and such activities can be conducted on an in-house or fee for service basis.

The minimum costs are those of subscription. To conduct it in-house has as its primary factor labor costs and the scope of material being analyzed, the number of newspapers, journals, etc. The great advantage of internal activity is complete control of the database and ready manipulation and integration with other issues identification and management tools.

We have no information on the cost of training in column inch counting or in the purchase of *ad hoc* services.

Summary. It is worth noting that this information is current and does not pretend to be tied to the three to five year emerging issues. However, it can be valuable to an issues manager. First, it does give a pulse of current issues. Second, it provides a model for quantification that can be expanded into other and earlier emerging issues. Third, in many organizations there is of necessity or by custom a commitment to the short-term and therefore the column inch counting technology is highly applicable to that situation.

Technique: Polls and Surveys

Polls are as American as cherry pie; and like cherry pie, they come in all varieties of quality, taste, and nutrition. The poll and survey have become so much a part of American life that no facet of it is without its relevant body of data. A major new national publication, *Public Opinion*, summarizes for an intelligent lay audience the latest survey results, often against a historical background. The more scholarly *Public Opinion Quarterly* has for decades been a primary reporter of techniques and survey results.

No large organization today can be indifferent to the results and value of survey research. The critical question is the extent to which one chooses to make a direct investment. The main choices are to rely on widely published material; to subscribe to specific proprietary studies; or to commission surveys.

A survey is a relatively expensive tool; but it invites disaster to be less than absolutely professional, using the best internal or external technical support one can afford. A badly constructed amateur survey is likely to be worse than no information at all.

The value of surveys lies, as with so many futures techniques, in coping with the increasing complexity of the corporate world. A survey can provide broad, reliable, quantitative information which can be conveniently disseminated, about societal developments, specific constituencies, and even one's own staff and workforce. Furthermore, the poll, if so designed, can help make a corporate plan or program credible to those very same groups.

The earliest and most common use of the survey by corporations was in market research. They have been extended to every corporate concern.

Surveys can tell us about broad shifts in public attitude. The well-known Harris Polls, for example, have shown a steady decline in public confidence in the corporation, the Congress, the military, medicine, higher education, and many other public institutions. Similarly, polls can be useful in showing changing consumer and worker attitudes, changing demands and public concerns dealing with health, safety, and the quality of the environment, or they can be targeted on specific or more localized affairs, the acceptability of a particular product change, or a particular civil or public endeavor.

A number of firms offer syndicated surveys, for example:

Firm	*Service*
Yankelovich, Skelly and White, Inc. New York, N.Y.	Corporate Priorities
Louis Harris and Associates, Inc. New York, N.Y.	Harris Perspective
Cambridge Reports, Inc. Cambridge, Mass.	The Cambridge Report
Opinion Research Corp. Princeton, N.J.	Public Opinion Index
The Roper Organization, Inc. New York, N.Y.	Roper Reports
Dresner, Morris and Tortorello New York, N.Y.	Viewpoint

Other organizations specialize in regional surveys. Many of the survey organizations will permit an add-on question for a client at $1,000 or less per question.

Fairly expensive general surveys, running from $10,000 to $30,000, can bring great insight and useful background information to an organization. But their very strength is also their weakness. They lack specificity or saliency to particular corporate concerns. For greater saliency one can move to tracking studies, studies which may be repeated over extended periods. For example, General Electric, through Trendex of Westport, Connecticut, has conducted quarterly surveys of 2,000 adults and 1,000 college students annually since 1965, addressing national issue questions. Dow Chemical has for a long time had similar surveys; trade associations such as the American Petroleum Institute and the National Agricultural Chemical Association conduct periodic tracking studies.

At the finest grain level are the so-called project studies, which are generally one-shot; for example, Sentry Insurance Company, through Louis Harris and Associates, surveyed 5,000 people in five countries on attitudes about productivity.

An important population for surveys are people close to the company; Public Service Company of Colorado mailed a survey questionnaire to all its shareholders. The Monsanto Company has surveyed its workforce and has changed some management practices as a result. In many cases, the company's workforce is representative of the general population, in addition to having a particular affiliation to the company. An organization may test a potential public outreach or public affairs program with its own employees. Obviously, if they laugh at a company program or respond negatively or harshly to it, it is hardly likely to go over with the public. A survey of one's workforce can build esprit, particularly if the use of the survey is clear to the staff.

The accumulation of survey data available publicly and through the syndicated surveys is a mountain of information to be mined any time.

As with most other information, the survey does not speak for itself, but the results of the survey must be analyzed, interpreted, and effectively delivered to the corporate clientele if it is to have any significant effect. Without that kind of interpretation, it becomes just another thing, or at best, some form of semi-professional entertainment.*

Time. With purchased survey and poll data, the principal commitment to time is in the interpretation of the results in terms of the company or organization's interests. That interpretation may involve relating the results

---

* This section on polls draws heavily on an article by R.D. Zentner, in Nagelschmidt's book. Zentner was Advisor on Issues Analysis to the Shell Oil Company. See Bibliography.

to earlier surveys and accumulated database, expert interpretation, or other hands-on, labor intensive devices. One must keep in mind in terms of almost any purchased service that the data do not speak for themselves. Although in interpretation time is the principal commitment, on the other hand, in the case of commissioned surveys, a great deal of time will be consumed in defining the questions and the issues; selecting the survey organization; framing questions jointly with the organization; and test and evaluation. Presumably, one would, with this investment, have an even richer and hence greater commitment to interpretation of the results.

Summary. Survey data can be an important part of any issues management program; it should be integrated into the scanning, identification, and monitoring of issues and used to test policies. First, familiarize people with public opinion data from public sources. Move on from there to one of the standard survey services. Be sure to integrate the information into interpretations of major company interests. On a key issue, test the water by doing your own survey. As a rule of thumb, to get a high level of confidence in the results, survey 1,200 to 1,500 people. Finally, do not rely on a single snapshot of attitude or opinion.

Technique: Jury of Executive Opinion

Panels of senior executives are a very widely used technique in issues management. They are, in the large and very large corporations, a most important element in issues management. The importance of panels of senior executives lies in two facts. First, they have the most intimate knowledge of the organization and hence lend great credibility to the opinions or conclusions which are drawn. Closely related and derivative of that is the fact that senior executives have great credibility in selectively pushing key issues forward to the very top management. The second value in panels of senior executives is that as the heads of the operating arms of the organization they will have primary responsibility for the implementation of any issues management program; and consequently, their early involvement in management of the emerging issue makes any necessary action more credible and actionable to them.

Sometimes the executive panel is a subset of the executive committee. In extremely large and complex organizations there often is an intermediary panel of second tier executives, who do some pre-processing, sorting, extensive background work, and so on, in preparation of materials to be sent to the executive committee. Those details are relatively unimportant, since they are an obvious consequence of the size of an operation.

The executive committees can serve several distinct functions:

- The identification of issues.

- The screening and evaluation of potential issues or issue candidates put before them from below.

- Setting priorities among issues.

- The assignments of responsibilities for managing the issue. This may include assignment to line officers, the formation of *ad hoc* task forces, or the direction to an issues management office or to a staff function such as consumer affairs, government affairs, etc.

- Monitoring progress in managing the issue.

- Receiving, reviewing, evaluating, and recommending actions coming from task forces, line managers, or staff offices.

- Preparation of the case for final decision by the President, CEO, or the Board.

Any or all of these functions are appropriate for the executive committee. One which is both difficult and valuable is using the executive committee to identify the issues. Generally, senior executives, by the time they reach that level, are literally unaccustomed and unpracticed in the generative and proposal side of work. Their primary organizational function is evaluation, disposal and allocation rather than generation and proposal. The reality of much of top management's corporate life is that they receive materials in a prefabricated, pre-evaluated format, which is often ideal for dealing with the large numbers of issues which do rise to their attention.

In many large organizations the preparation of materials for senior managers is an important administrative organizational art form. However, by the nature of the case, emerging issues are vague and uncertain in their development, and unclear in their significance and implications for the organization. Techniques, therefore, which inadvertently force them into more crisp or precise categories can be misleading. Emerging issues may call for special treatment in their presentation to the very top executives. Consequently, experience such as that at Monsanto has found the direct use of executive committees to be laborious and time consuming. However, the compensatory value, education, cannot be gotten at as well by any other mechanism. The executive committee, by working to define issues, forces understanding of the process of thinking through the whole issues identification and management cycle. It is an unbeatable learning experience for the members. Consequently, a plausible step is to have the executive committee, at least in year one, be active in the identification and shaping of the issues.

On the business of assignment of responsibilities, the sense from our interviews is that issues management is best performed by those with the most relevant line responsibilities. This is not always desirable or practical. For example, a public or consumer affairs office may be the best place to handle some issues, particularly the truly short-term, zero to one year issues. On the other hand, many of the implications of an emerging issue belong in the hands of the strategic planning office.

The central function which no other unit except the president can perform is the tieing of a reward structure, a compensation structure, to taking on and effectively dealing with issues identification, scanning, monitoring, and management. One of the surest indicators that the senior management is concerned with an activity is that people involved in that activity are selectively rewarded. Consequently, an effective indicator of a company's concern for the identification of emerging issues and their effective handling by senior managers and others throughout the organization is the relating of that process of compensation to the effectiveness in dealing with the emerging issue. In an ideal situation the emerging issues concerns would become an explicit factor in the evaluation of the performance of senior and middle managers throughout the company or organization. The executive committee can have a critical role in defining the relationship between the identification and management of issues and expected performance of middle and upper managers.

The executive committee as well as the president, and even the board, can have special knowledge which other members of the organization are likely to be ignorant of. For example, if a unit is to be sold, or abandoned, an important emerging issue in relation to it may merit little attention. If an issue would be seriously modified by a proposed acquisition, that may modify what would be otherwise a fully rational issues management plan. In a very large organization, a common technique, for example as used at AT&T, is to have second tier managers participate in a issues identification function with the Director of Issues Management. Working with the scanning and monitoring and other externally and internally produced material, they do the first cut issues identification and the first cut assignments for the data gathering and the preparation of initial materials for the executive committee. As a practical note, whoever is in charge as the coordinator or key person in issues identification must be closely attentive to the care and feeding of executive committees.

With regard to membership organizations such as trade associations, panels of executives often play a key role in issues identification. As, for example, in the Public Affairs Council, the National Association of Manufacturers, and the Chemical Manufacturers Association. These are valuable functions in membership organizations.

Time and Cost. Time of senior managers is one of the most precious resources of any large organization. The costs associated with the use of that time are not easily monetized. Furthermore, many senior managers recognize and handle their time as a highly limited resource. It is essential, therefore, that any system set up involving senior managers pay close attention to planning and preparation for the use of senior managers' time in an optimal way. For example, an issues manager in one organization points out that of the several hundred issues that the issues identification process may be considering at any one time, only four or five are brought to the active attention of the senior managers. In other organizations the number may be as high as a dozen or two.

Summary. Committees of senior executives, preferably the executive committee itself, are indispensable elements to an issues management program. Use them.

Technique: Expert Panels

Expert panels are used and useful in many aspects of issues management. The problems are: Who is an expert? And experts for what purpose?

The expert panel can be used to explore, to train, to evaluate, to certify, or to build a constituency. These are not mutually exclusive uses. But the objective of an expert panel ought to be clearly in mind before going to the expense of recruiting outside experts.

Many organizations use internal experts, either in panel or meeting format, or more generally in a task force. The internal uses of task forces for many purposes are quite extensive in organizations like Allied Chemical, IBM, and Xerox.

The key problem in the selection of the expert panel on an issue has to do with the fact that most issues have elements which exceed the expertise of any traditional specialist. If one were dealing with a water pollution problem, the most serious error one might make would be to draw solely upon hydrologists and sanitarians. One must bring in people from state and local government, those trained in policy identification, toxicology, public administration, consumer affairs, and government affairs, to form an *ad hoc* expert pool.

One of the reported benefits of experts is that they will often bring fresh insights and raise new aspects to an issue even though they may be brought together for a more narrow technical purpose.

Another aspect to the expert panel is to salt them into a panel of your own experts. One or two outsiders bring a complementary perspective. This is institutionalized in some of the issues scanning services as available through, for example, Weiner Edrich Brown, Inc., who bring together their own expertise with their clients' to form a panel in discussing scanning issues. The TAP program of the American Council of Life Insurance, in discussing its own clippings and gleanings among their staff experts, routinely brings in a professional futurist to add an outside perspective.

Another aspect of the expert panel use, which in some regards is lower cost than the assembly on site, is the use of the conversational Delphi, described elsewhere in this section.

Time and Cost. Time and cost in the use of outside experts or expert panels is clearly not in the cost of the expertise but in the internal staff time required to service the outside experts. To bring them up to speed on the problem as perceived or defined by the company, and to work with them effectively all incur substantially large internal cost compared to the cost of the experts' time. When tied to purchase of other services, the use of outside experts tends to be channeled through only one or two people, and there is great discretion in whether internal staff even participates in the face-to-face expert meetings associated with those services.

Summary. Outside experts are useful but they will never substitute for the internal hard thinking required to frame and shape an issue, explore the alternatives, and evaluate the action options.

Technique: Scanning and Monitoring

The text in Chapter 2, pages 30 through 36 discusses scanning and monitoring in detail.

The reader should note the summary evaluation of scanning and monitoring in Figure 3-1.

Technique: Content Analysis

Content analysis is a technique developed in the 1930s, widely employed in World War II, and now a mainstay of the national security establishment's international intelligence system. The technique depends upon several well validated assumptions:

- First, public and private material printed, broadcast, published, written, or disseminated for one purpose often carries along with it information relevant to another topic. Implicit information is often more reliable and honest than direct, purposefully presented data.

- Second, such information can be identified, segregated, codified, analyzed, and usefully interpreted. There are patterns to such information which respond in ways that reflect the current situation, anticipate unfolding trends, or reveal real, deep-seated attitudes.

- Third, in many cases, the results of content analysis will correlate with, shed light on, or test information coming from other sources.

The technique is conceptually straightforward and elementary. The skill lies in the detail, continuity, the scope of effort, the willingness to invest in the time and labor, and the ability to interpret.

The best known current practitioner of content analysis is the Naisbitt Group, which monitors about 6,000 individual issues in some 200 newspapers monthly, as well as other publications. Its proprietary services include the Trend Report and four regional reports dealing with California, the Rocky Mountains, Florida, and the Midwest. Other organizations, such as PR Data Systems of Wilton, Connecticut and the News Analysis Institute of Pittsburgh, specialize in content analysis. Private organizations such as Hill and Knowlton, Inc., a public relations firm, now do content analysis.

The technique depends upon close reading of specified sources and sorting into pre-established coding categories. This provides both the content, that is, the meaning, and the opportunity to quantify results. Figure 3-3 shows how a very simple category of favorable and unfavorable press coverage might be monitored by content analysis. It is interesting to note that AT&T, beginning in 1976, used content analysis to monitor public attitudes toward its operating companies.

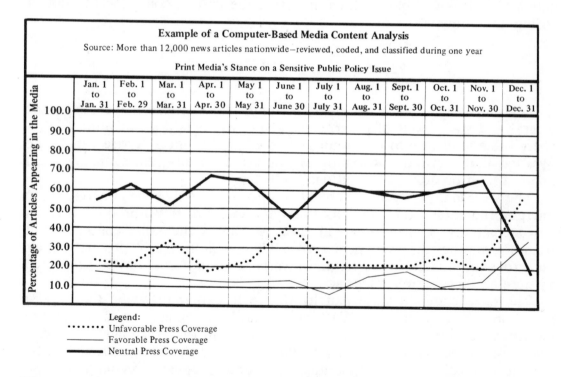

Figure 3-3. Example of a Computer-Based Media Content Analysis

Source: Walter K. Lindenmann, "Content Analysis," *Public Relations Journal*, July 1983, p. 25.

The technique is not limited to newspapers. Any form of communication may be monitored—television, novels, fiction, speeches, whatever. For example, one analyst has done a content analysis of Presidential inaugural addresses, calculating an index of orientation toward the future of the last six Presidents of the United States.

The use of the technique depends upon a long-time commitment. Consequently, it is not a technique to be undertaken impetuously or lightly. Otherwise the effort is likely to be completely wasted. The technique lends itself to local, regional, national, and international analyses.

The concept is closely allied to the notion of Precursor Analysis or bellwether regions; a variant is described under Media Analysis.

Cost. Cost varies enormously. A broadsweeping national or regional analysis such as the Naisbitt Trend Report gives quarterly reports in thirteen major categories at $1,250 annually. Individual company based content analysis would be much more costly, being labor intensive in both collection and interpretation. There are numerous clipping services available on state, national, and topical bases which moderate the cost of collection but not of coding and analysis.

Technique: Legislative Tracking

Legislative scanning is extremely popular. As practiced it focuses on the federal and state levels of government primarily. It is done at almost every conceivable level of effort by many kinds of practitioners. There can be no question that legislative scanning is important to any issues management program in a broadly based national industry.

The regionally based company is not the only one interested in intergovernmental, state, and local level affairs. A multi-product broadly based company, such as General Electric, shares the same concerns, but from a somewhat different perspective. Their wide range of products, their numerous manufacturing sites, and divergent labor force may be impacted by state and local government actions.

The most common variety of legislative tracking, involving the biggest labor force, is the activity of Washington and State House representatives of individual corporations and trade associations, and the Washington lobbyist. They will not be discussed to any extent in this report. They concentrate on current legislation, i.e., impending bills and proposed regulations, and attempt to understand and influence voting that will affect their interests. From an issues point of view, the Washington representatives' attention is on those items now on the front burner. Issues management deals with the attempt to identify those issues which will emerge over the next two to seven years and be important to the company or to the industry. This present discussion is on the longer-term perspectives.

Depending on the complexity of the matter and the type of corporation, there is an active and useful role for in-house legislative scanning, for trade, professional, and business associations scanning, and commercial services.

Perhaps the oldest legislative monitoring system is the Congressional Research Service, which is an agency at the Library of Congress. It is the information arm of the Congress and a research unit, producing a variety of different reports. Consequently, tieing into the Congressional Research Service information base is a worthwhile activity. Policy Analysis Company, Inc., in Washington, D.C., has tied into that process in two interesting ways, offering commercial services.

Congress Scan identifies the evolving issues by monitoring the production of materials by the Congressional Research Service. It is premised on the notion of trigger events being discernible in terms of the information requests generated by Congressmen or Congressional committees, and responded to by the Congressional Research Service (CRS). One important event in that pattern is the release of an Issue Paper by CRS. This implies, as a minimum, that they have received or expect many Congressional requests on the subject.

The staff of CRS, however, also performs tailor-made studies at the request of a Congressman. Those studies are strictly confidential in terms of the topic and the requesting member. However, the individual Congressman, after receiving a report, may decide to release it, to make it generally available, or to make it available on a limited basis. When those individual requests become available and are assigned numbers, they present a visible sign of interest in an emerging issue. For example, there are some five of these specially requested papers, not yet part of the issues paper system, dealing solely with questions on ethylene dibromide. This source of information affords an effective early warning on emerging short-term Congressional interests. *Congress Scan* tracks all of this. The service is available at the cost of $200 per year per topical interest.

LegiScan, in contrast to *Congress Scan*, is a major research based service. The Policy Analysis Company has a framework of 67 issues that it works with, premised on the widely documented observation that the latent period, the period of buildup, fermentation, and maturation within the Congress can run as few as five, and as long as thirty, years. The *LegiScan* concept is based upon monitoring and analyzing the "quiet zone," this long interval from first activity to final legislation. It depends upon the analysis of proposed bills. For example, in one study, 9,000 bills were analyzed, covering 45 issue areas. In the area of housing alone, some 900 bills were reviewed. Understanding the pattern of content of these bills gives one great insight into the emerging Congressional deliberations; at least, that is the working hypothesis.

The use of such services helps to set a specific agenda, let us say, for the Washington office of a corporation or trade association. They educate top management and offer insight into emerging issues. An example of that insight: one can easily believe that the proposing of a bill by a senior member of the committee is an important benchmark activity. That alone, however, is not sufficient. In order for a bill to have any chance of moving forward and becoming legislation, it must have an institutionalized base and not be merely a personal interest of a member, however important he or she is. An illustration of the limitation of personal interest is the strong concern that Congressman Van Deerlin had for telecommunications reform. He even managed to acquire two hundred Congressional signatures requesting actions to revise the Communications Act of 1934. But that interest had no institutional setting, and, consequently, it never came to much in spite of a great deal of personal interest by an influential member of the Congress.

LegiScan costs $7,200 per year for a subscription to 20 of the 67 issues. The client receives a single package on each issue.

Computerized legislative information services are performed by the *Commerce Clearinghouse* in Chicago, *Public Affairs Inflow* of Sacramento, California, and *Legislate*, recently bought by the *Washington Post*. *Legislate* had been limited to federal level information, but is rumored to be moving to state level material.

The need to understand the complexities of state level policy is being met by a variety of evolving information and advisory services.

As noted earlier, we found very little going on by way of formal services in the international area. A newsletter, *International Policy*, is put out by the National Center for Legislative Research.

Summary. Virtually every organization has some kind of governmental affairs office at the state or federal level. What is needed and is emphasized in this section are techniques and services which address the emerging issues earlier and which allow a company in a particular city, county, state, or region to get earlier insights into what may be happening in its own jurisdiction and may be happening in other jurisdictions that will eventually impact on it. In our judgment, this is the most primitive and complex of the issues management areas, but one with very high payoff for some industries, the electric utility industry, for example. As a nationwide but highly distributed industry influenced by state and local legislation and regulation and numerous public interest groups, the awareness of what is happening in one region is likely to have great early warning value for utilities in other regions or districts. The benefits of legislative tracking here closely parallel the benefits already discussed of bellwether jurisdictions and precursor analysis.

Technique: Delphi

This survey technique uses a panel of experts to judge the timing, probability, importance, and implications of factors, trends, and events with regard to the subject under consideration.

The Delphi technique was developed in response to several difficulties encountered when formal meetings of experts are convened: high costs, the inevitable unavailability of some specialists, bandwagon effects, and the implicit or explicit dominance of high prestige or especially articulate panel members. The latter problem is particularly important because one or more panel members are often reluctant to challenge directly the opinion of a majority of their peers.

Key Features. The Delphi technique developed at the Rand Corporation has become the most popular forecasting technique generally used in the United States by public and private institutions. Thousands of Delphi surveys have been made. The most elaborate ever published was an internal Delphi done by TRW for corporate planning purposes; the printed version weighed 19 pounds. This popularity hinges upon the fact that almost any subject or question can be treated. Quantitative results are obtained. The technique captures the judgment of experts or of parties at interest.

The Delphi technique, as originally designed, involves a multistep process. Responses to each question on a Delphi are arrayed along a range or continuum. For example, a question about when solar energy will become economically competitive with petroleum for specific purposes might elicit answers ranging from 1990 to "never." The range of responses is divided into quartiles, and those whose responses fall in one of the quartiles at either extreme along the range are asked to justify their answers by stating their assumptions or describing their reasoning. These justifications are then communicated, along with the full range of answers, to all of the respondents, and they are asked to answer the original questions for a second round of the Delphi. The process is then repeated for a third round. The usual result is that the responses converge toward a consensus point, or a narrow range, which is considered more likely to be an accurate forecast than that of an individual expert.

This elaborate process is now often simplified or truncated to one or two rounds. This appears to produce results of about the same quality as the more costly and time consuming original process. In the early Delphis, large panels running to scores, even hundreds, of participants were used. In the current practice, two rounds involving usually 10-20 people are considered sufficient.

A Delphi survey is almost always handled by mail. When well designed, a Delphi should take no more than 30 minutes of the respondent's time for each round.

Uses. Delphi is generally used when high premium is put on judgment rather than on new or substantive information gathered by other more formal literature or survey techniques.

The technique has expanded to permit comparisons among subsets of experts and between experts and non-expert populations, especially interested or affected parties.

Implicit in the process are the limitations on the reliability of the judgments, and the qualifications or commitment of participants. This limitation leads to the primary abuse of Delphi, which is to confuse its responses with "answers." Delphi is best used as an input to a larger forecasting and futures process. It produces judgmental evaluation, or estimates of probabilities, not objective or factual information. However, the fact that results are quantitative, can be broadly based, and can be displayed in attractive formats, frequently beguiles sponsors into confusing this input tool with an output tool.

Several key points are important in designing a Delphi questionnaire:

- The preparation of the questionnaire and the establishment of useful, effective, unambiguous questions is the critical labor input into the preparation of the Delphi. Failure at this stage is the primary cause of weak, uncertain, or useless results.

- Questions need not be limited to text questions. The respondents may be asked to carry a trend line into the future, or engage in other variations of graphic representation.

- Extensive research on Delphi, using almanac type information as surrogates for future outcomes, shows that a Delphi works best when the pool of panelists collectively has large amounts of information about the subject, even though that information may be fragmented and disparate. The results may range over several orders of magnitude, differing by factors as much as a million, when the group is ignorant of and has few intellectual hooks into the subject.

How to Set Up. A typical, well run Delphi procedure involves the following steps:

- Define the subject area to be explored by Delphi.

- Engage experienced practitioners in preparation of the Delphi questionnaire.

- Review available literature, information, judgment, opinion.

- Frame the Delphi survey. Note that in the survey questions, one almost always leaves open the opportunity for respondents to add items. For example, in a list of items being evaluated for likelihood and importance in affecting the future of cogeneration, one might list six or seven items, but leave blank spaces for the respondents to add three or four of their own and evaluate in similar fashion.

- Review, evaluate, modify, and dry run the survey with people informed about the topic, but not connected with its preparation.

- Iterate the above steps until satisfied.

- Identify the purpose in the selection of the survey sample. Is it intended, for example, to include only experts, only in-house experts, affected parties, hostile parties, public at large, etc.? Define the range and size of the sample.

- Network to identify the range of experts to be covered. Networking is a process by which, through telephone contacts starting with almost any knowledge base, one inquires as to who the experts in the field are and uses experts to identify other experts.

- Telephone or write to the panel to recruit their participation, define their responsibilities and the burden on them, how much time it will take, what the likely time cycle will be, and the *quid pro quo* for participation—normally access to the results. Rarely is an honorarium offered, expected, or required.

- Send out the first round.

- Review and evaluate, collate, and redistribute, including any special points meriting note in the second round survey.

- Iterate.

- Codify, represent, organize, interpret, and present results to the client for review and evaluation.

- Reinterpret, expand, and clarify findings.

- Deliver results to client and to participants.

Time. A Delphi operated by mail is very time consuming because of the delays in response time. You normally should allow the respondent two weeks to reply. There are inevitably delays in postal time—you must allow at least two weeks for receipt of the questionnaire and two weeks for return of responses. Therefore, each cycle takes a minimum of six weeks. You must also allow time for telephone or mail stimulation, particularly with a small sample, to be sure that a reasonable percentage of respondents reply.

The preparation time for the survey itself will often take several weeks, and the interpretation time several weeks. A convenient range around which to work is thus eighteen weeks.

Costs. Allowing for a modest sized panel and all the associated activities involved, we estimate $500 per participant is a fair aggregate number, assuming one is working with a commercial study house in planning, designing, executing, and servicing the Delphi. One can substantially cut those costs with in-house labor, but it is absolutely essential to use a skilled Delphi practitioner.

Advantages to the technique:

- A large pool of Delphis is available for comparison, examples, and baseline data.

- There are many models to draw upon and modify.

- Delphis can be contracted out or done internally.

- Costs are relatively low, and one time.

- The technique is easily understood, clear, and transferable.

- Computer assisted software is available.

- Database requirements are very low. Use materials at hand.

- Delphi is particularly good for organizations and associations with large constituencies. It gives broad outreach at relatively low cost.

- Delphi looks scientific.

- Delphi results can acquire the halo of authority merely on the basis of the broad participation.

- Delphi results can often be conveniently summarized in a page or two.

Disadvantages:

- The validity is low.

- The difficulty of framing questions effectively is high.

- The format is procrustean; it allows only limited expression of subtle judgments.

- Delphi results are often poorly presented.

Summary. Delphi is definitely not recommended when other alternatives are available such as the conversational Delphi. Conventional Delphi is a last resort, not a first choice.

Technique: *Conversational Delphi - The Structured Interview*

The limitations on the Delphi, lack of subtlety in feedback, the inability to readily get exposition on critical points and the procrustean nature of the questions, have led to a radical revision in the Delphi concept—the use of a Delphi type questionnaire in a structured interview.

Key Features. Much of the technique remains the same. One identifies the pool of experts by networking, sets up a structured discussion format based upon knowledge and information at the time of starting the project, and dry runs and reevaluates the format. The critical difference is that instead of mailout of a highly structured form one does face-to-face or extended telephone interviews.

In the face-to-face interview one does not just run down a checklist but rather goes through a series of leading questions, noting the responses. This permits the respondent to emphasize and amplify important points and throw other points into perspective; it allows for clarification. Each interview may contribute to making subsequent interviews more informal, subtle, and interactive. One normally preserves the anonymity of the participants.

It is also practical to recycle to the early interviewees in a follow-on telephone conversation with specific points needing clarification.

The face-to-face interview itself is best done by two people. One engages the discussion, the other is notetaker.

A strong consensus on the part of the people who have done this extensively is that it is unwise to audiotape the interview. In some cases it inhibits. It also doubles the work in that someone has to go back and listen to the tape again. Taping also tends to promote lax notetaking rather than sharp attentive notetaking.

Immediately after the interview it is best if the interviewer or pair of interviewers dump their notes into a tape recorder for subsequent transcription.

It is difficult to conduct more than two or three telephone or face-to-face interviews a day because of scheduling, notetaking, and the audio dump.

Uses. A further advantage of the structured interview is that you can use each interview as a point to identify other people in the network of experts who should be contacted. In other words, one need not have a fixed roster of interviewees at the beginning of the process.

Working with a topic requiring expert inputs, the interview technique is far more valuable than the traditional Delphi because it permits the probing of the topic in whatever detail is appropriate.

It is crucial again in dealing with the expert situation that the interviewers be as well-informed as time and their own skills permit. One does not want to enter an interview with experts at a totally mismatched level of preparation.

Time. The sit-down, face-to-face interviews can comfortably run thirty to sixty minutes. If things seem to be going well and it suits the interviewee and the topic is rich enough, they may become quite open-ended. Running to two hours is not unusual.

In the telephone interview it is difficult to hold someone for more than thirty minutes. Sixty minutes is a really practical ultimate limit. With the telephone one is often much more crisp in having a series of points that one can go over. Just the fact that it is a more structured medium permits one to introduce more structure into the telephone interview than into the face-to-face.

The critical features in either format are the dry run and practice by the interviewers before launching into any of the interviews.

Substantially less time is required than a mail Delphi, since one has no dead time required as in each of the rounds of mailings and return receipts. Aside from the direct interview time, realistically two interviews per day, the major time blocks are in the startup planning, preparation, literature review, the framing of the issues and time to write the report.

Costs. Costs are comparable to a traditional Delphi. One can handle a thirty person interview pool for approximately thirty to forty thousand dollars; if one goes to the telephone format that would be reduced by about half.

Additional Comments. A number of techniques can be used in the face-to-face interview which are impractical by either telephone or traditional Delphi. For example:

- In one study of international conflict we presented interviewers with a global map and asked them to identify sites of conflict in the next 25 years and rank order them. The map was a useful reminder.

- Assume one has developed a set of events or factors affecting the situation under consideration. One can put each of these factors on a separate 3 X 5 card and have the interviewee place them in order, the most important cards on the top to least important on the bottom. One can even provide blank cards for filler space if the interviewee feels there is a big jump between some of the items. The forced choice works extremely well and can be done in a few minutes.

- A variation is to have the interviewee sort cards in a two-dimensional array on the desk top, let's say in terms of imminence and importance, imminence being left to right, importance being top to bottom. One can then carry on a structured discussion of the elements laid out in that matrix.

Summary. Whenever practical the face-to-face structured interview is the preferred mode of dealing with matters of expert opinion and judgment.

Technique: The Consensor

The Consensor is an electronic device which can profoundly influence small group interaction and response to an issue under discussion. The basic arrangement consists of a group of, let us say, sixteen people around a table. Each has a small hand-held device with scoring dial and a registration button. The person running the meeting is at the head of the table where there is a screen, very much resembling a video game backboard or a TV monitor. As the discussion proceeds the chairman will call the question. For example, "On a scale of one to ten the principal market for this product will be ———." Then he can go through individual market components and get the group's score on each.

In terms of presentation, and only when everyone has registered by setting the dial and pressing the button, a histogram appears showing the distribution of those votes. The special feature of the Consensor is that it permits a completely anonymous response in a group meeting. Assuming that the person in charge in fact wishes to get full frank honest responses from the group, the technique is extremely effective. One can literally go through scores of questions in a brief meeting, shaping and reshaping, evaluating and reevaluating the issues milieu in the responses. Should someone object that a question is incorrectly or badly formed or finds the responses incredible, that person may formulate the question his way and instantly test it with the group.

One of the incidental benefits of the use of the Consensor that has been noted in some contexts, is that individuals in the group who thought that they alone had an uncongenial opinion, that is, one uncongenial to the orientation of the group, will frequently find that others share the opinion.

The device is expensive, although it can be rented at a fairly stiff daily fee. It is recommended only to those groups who will be making fairly frequent use of it. There are several commercial variations on the device.

The Consensor has a strong play element to it. People are engaged very much by the device, and its operation is simple and straightforward enough that various individuals in a group can assume the chairman role and operate the equipment on a rotational basis if that fits the ambience of the group.

The Consensor is marketed by Applied Futures, Inc., Greenwich, Connecticut 06830.

Technique: Cross Impact Analysis

Many techniques for probing the future implicitly or explicitly assume little or no interaction from other trends or events. Yet it is apparent that the interactions can be as important as a particular trend itself. Cross impact analysis was developed to help understand how new developments or trends could affect each other.

As a technique, it can be applied at an elementary qualitative level by an individual or by a group. It can be used with a relatively simple computer assisted program such as KSIM* , or it can become the basis for a quite detailed, intensive, quantitative analysis. The technique is easily grasped from the elementary or qualitative point of view.

How it Works. Assume, merely as a basis of discussion, that the subject at hand is application of photovoltaics to individual homes. Assume on the basis of some previous analysis, the following four trends or events have been identified as important:

A. A 60% decrease in the cost of photovoltaic cells.

B. Costs in traditional electrical power rise 70%.

C. Number of housing starts.

D. Movement toward more uniform housing and construction codes at the local government level.

One sets up a 4 X 4 Matrix:

Effects of Event

	A	B	C	D
A	X			
B		X		
C			X	
D				X

Effects of Event

---

* KSIM is a software package for a highly simplified systems dynamic model. It permits an analyst in real time to take the variables identified in cross impact analysis, assign them functions within the model and quickly trace out time histories of the variables under discussion. KSIM is a real time tool for small group interactions, in which the implications of assumptions are readily tested. Its primary value is exploratory, not analytical. (See J. Kane.)

- Then one asks these questions, in turn: Assume event A occurs, how will it affect the likelihood of B, C, and D? Positively, very positively, not at all, negatively, or very strongly negatively? Those judgments are designated as (+), (++), (O), (-), and (—). Similarly, if B comes to pass, how it will affect the likelihood of A, C, and D, and so forth? By this method, one clarifies one's judgments. In a group, one can then compare individual judgments and develop significant discussion around those alleged interactions. Therefore cross impact is used to explore the assumptions and to identify significant points of divergence and agreement. In this use it can be the driver of further directed study, evaluation, and research.

The next stage in complexity, applicable in small groups, ties a cross impact analysis to some interactive computer tool such as KSIM. The outputs of the cross impact matrix become the input to a simple real time modeling program. This more dynamic, rapid interaction among the variables permits immediate generation and evaluation of any assumptions that the group believes, disbelieves, or chooses to explore.

The application of cross impact analysis in a more thorough quantitative way is a substantial intellectual, analytical, and time-consuming process. For example, it has been practiced at Monsanto Chemical Company in looking at how a set of technical marketing and competitive variables enter into chemical manufacturing process choices. A group of experts would meet, with a large amount of technical data in hand, to develop mathematical relationships for each cell of the matrix (which can easily run to 20 X 20).

The technique is more frequently used in a qualitative than in a quantitative mode. It is not a technique which one casually uses and drops. It is a technique which becomes part of a larger system, which must be congenial to the ambience of an organization.

Cross impact has been employed as a relatively elementary low cost planning tool. At the other extreme, the University of Southern California's Center for Futures Research has made it a part of their sophisticated INTERAX program (Interactive Cross Impact Simulation). INTERAX is a forecasting procedure that uses both analytic models and human analysis to develop a better understanding of alternative future environments. It does this by generating scenarios one year at a time so that policy makers can interact with each scenario as it is being generated to experiment with policy options. INTERAX contains data needed to analyze a wide range of strategic issues in a computer model that can also be linked to existing corporate models.

The full INTERAX program has been developed and made operational. The program consists of a computerized cross impact model and database, as well as an operations manual describing how to add other events and trends to the cross impact model, how to run the model interactively to generate scenarios, and how to couple the cross impact model to other models. The database contains detailed data on several hundred events and trends, of which 100 events and 50 trends are incorporated in the model along with estimates of probability distributions and cross impact factors. The program has been implemented and is currently in operation at 13 major U.S. corporations.

Work on INTERAX has led to updating and expanding the database and creating an INTERAX Users Association to facilitate the exchange of user experience. Whether basic or complex, the purpose is the same: to get at assumptions, explore relationships, and use it as a tool for further development of those interrelationships. The cross impact technique can also be used in Decision Support Systems (see that technique description) to define the range of significant inputs going into a spreadsheet analysis. Reciprocally, a spreadsheet analysis can suggest the range of variables that one would wish to explore in a cross impact analysis.

Cross impact illustrates a common feature of futures tools: they rarely stand alone but are best used as a part of a continuing chain of interactive processes.

Costs. Cross impact can have no marginal costs if done as a desktop tool by an individual. If done as a group, it costs no more than the group's meeting time. If the semi-quantitative techniques involving something like KSIM are employed, the costs are then for KSIM equipment which presumably is an overhead item frequently used.

The cost can move up in using it in the detailed quantitative way, as in the Monsanto planning experience. A great deal of background data, intense activity at day-long or more than day-long planning sessions, and elaborate follow-through to clarify a critical point are all expensive. Finally, if one moves to something like INTERAX, that model plus a couple of days in training comes at a fixed price of $14,500. Obviously, operating costs are equivalently high.

Summary. Cross impact analysis is a very valuable tool available at a wide range of sophistication, complexity, and backup requirements. It might be best to attempt to use cross impact without any computer assisted techniques to become familiar with the concept, and then move into semi-quantitative applications such as KSIM, and finally give attention to the more elaborate and expensive applications.

Technique: *Decision Support Systems*

Decision Support Systems (DSS) is a new jargon term reflecting the emerging major changes that computer technology will have on strategic planning and strategic management. According to Ralph Sprague, DSS are characterized as "interactive computer based systems, which help decision-makers utilize data and models to solve unstructured problems." In some sense it is a logical progression from EDP, electronic data processing, which is focused on data, to MIS, management information systems, which primarily have an information focus. Now DDS has a decision focus.

The concept reflects the rapidly evolving new capabilities and the integration of micro and mainframe computers with software and databases. The new capabilities provide for quick, flexible real time manipulation of assumptions to determine consequences. Perhaps the most successful and widespread current application of the DSS concept is in the linkage of databases with spreadsheets, now widely available for microcomputers. This permits the exploration of assumptions and the determination almost immediately of spreadsheet implications of those assumptions. There is a reverse benefit. Exploring areas where new data can usefully and productively be gathered further ratchets up the analytical capabilities. DSS seems to be rapidly moving past being merely a new buzzword to a significant step ahead in adaptive decision-making applicable to complex judgmental situations of a true management sort.

Some Details. The Decision Support System simulates business decisions mathematically and predicts the results from pursuing one course of action versus another. The effectiveness of these systems is dependent on the ability to define and quantify the variables. Significant results have been achieved in using Decision Support Systems in financial planning, portfolio analysis, tax planning, and market analysis.

Decision Support Systems are a combination of hardware or computer software programs and people. They may be tied into a database management system and data communications systems, or they may be very independent mini-micro systems, or they may bring together all the components of the management information systems.

The value for issues management lies in the fact that typical accounting oriented transaction data can be supplemented with nontransactional, nonaccounting data from inside or outside, some of which has not been computerized in the past.

Data extraction and database management systems must be flexible enough to allow rapid additions and changes in response to unanticipated user requests. Some successful systems have found it necessary to create a database for the DSS which is logically separate from other operational databases.

The key capabilities for a DSS in the model subsystem include:

- The ability to create new models quickly and easily.

- The ability to catalog and maintain a wide range of models and interrelate these models with appropriate linkage through the database.

- The ability to manage the model base with management functions analogous to database management.

User friendly packages to create a DSS require a high level of skill in their preparation. The software aids include:

- File construction.

- A report generator.

- A graphic presentation.

- Select modeling packages including financial and statistical analysis.

If the user is sophisticated and knowledgeable, he or she can create trend lines and do trend permutation. But DSS can be more than trending and simulation. Understanding and manipulating the mathematical formulation and assumptions built into packages is the heart of the decision analysis.

Decision Support Systems are tools which assist rather than replace critical decision-making. The manager still makes the decision. The interactive computer based systems help decision-makers use data and models to solve unstructured problems, i.e., problems which have no programmable procedures, as in strategic planning and often in issues management.

Because strategic decisions are made by groups of managers, there is no universally accepted model of the decision-making process. Variability in the characteristics of decision-makers is added to the many variables and different types of decisions. As a result, one of the important characteristics of a DSS is that it provides the decision-makers with a set of capabilities to apply in a sequence and form that fits each individual style. Therefore, DSS is process independent and user driven and controlled.

The rapid growth in Decision Support Systems as an aid to organizational decision-making is reflected in the establishment of a new journal, *Decision Support Systems*, edited by Andrew Whinston of Purdue University and Hans-Jochen Schneider of the Technical University of Berlin. The new journal purports to integrate the computer science and management science aspects of this emerging area. The publisher is Elsevier.

Summary. Decision Support Systems will, under this or another name, become a routine adjunct of strategic and operational planning in most organizations. In the current stage of issues management, DSS ought not be an early or primary target of attention and development in starting a program. It should be anticipated as a tool to be acquired and used as issues management systems evolve.

Technique: Computer Assisted Techniques

The computer is a tool applicable to and in fact used in planning in most large organizations. Rucks and Ginter, in a survey of 4,000 members of the Planning Executives Institute (for which they had a 24% effective response) showed extremely high use of computers in strategic modeling and simulation. Fifty-one percent of the respondents reported models or simulations were used in their strategic planning process. And of those models, 94% were computer based.

With regard to the techniques more directly applicable to issues management, see the previous discussion of Decision Support Systems (DSS). The widespread application of spreadsheet analysis depends upon low cost, conveniently available microcomputers or accessible consoles to mainframes, coupled with computer assisted databases and suitable software packages.

Other techniques such as Delphi can be enormously enhanced by a simple computer analytical program. Trend extrapolation can certainly be accomplished with the assistance of computers. New interactive flexible computer programs carry that a step further and permit alternative assumptions about future trends to create a family of trend extrapolations very rapidly, literally while one watches.

Holloway and Pearce, in their comments on computer assisted strategic planning, point out that the key and far reaching capability is to simulate all major steps in the corporate planning process, and to identify planning constraints and resource requirements, to a degree if not technically at least practically impossible by manual methods:

Environmental forecasts, consolidated internal data, strategic planning simulation of one-year linear programming models, and multi-year programming models can all be usefully integrated into planning.

One particular sectionalized computer assisted strategic planning system contained environmental forecasts, consolidated internal data, a strategic planning simulation model, a 1-year linear programming model and a multi-year linear programming model. The objective of environmental forecast modeling is to provide the user with the facility for maintaining, evaluating, and adjusting a computer database. The corporate database provides, in printed form, a manual reference document. It is also a consistent pool of information from which all computer models can proceed.

The main purpose of a computer simulation model is to generate guidelines for company-wide growth and adaptation to environmental change. It is an aid for management decisions as well as a tool for developing broad strategies. Its output is in six sections—input data, calculated results-consolidated strategic Business Unit summary, base case calculated results by functional area, base case calculated results by profit centre, product movements projected by base case, and a financial summary.

There is another way to use the tool. This is called the Monte Carlo method. Possible events or values of essential factors, such as markets and breakthroughs in R&D, are set down together with the probabilities associated with their occurrence. Simulation is in fact a tool for providing reasonable answers from limited data. In the case of the multi-year linear programming model, the computer capacity for speedy multi-dimensional multi-purpose and complex forecasts facilitates the use of comprehensive relevant data for both strategic and operational decision-making. Linear programming is very powerful where large masses of interrelated data must be carried and manipulated. Thus a combination of simulation and linear programming provides an excellent long-term planning system.

The application of computer and telecommunications technologies to issues identification tracking and monitoring will become increasingly important. For the moment, in a startup operation these techniques are likely to be irrelevant; if too aggressively pursued, a distraction; or at best, a marginal convenience. The problems in startup issues identification tracking and monitoring have more to do with the characteristics of the corporate culture, designing and fitting the system to people involved, and intense, intimate hands-on interaction with people. Insofar as telecommunications and computers become a distraction, they are a step backward from that objective.

On the other hand, there can be no question that the revolution in office automation and the intense pace of acquisition of office automation and information systems will transform relationships within and between organizations. Consequently, it is essential that an issues management system be framed with a view to phasing into this technology and taking advantage of it.

The importance of this family of technologies for issues management lies even more in seeing it as a source of issues than in seeing it merely as a tool for understanding those issues. Information technology is used here in the broadest sense to embrace everything from microprocessors to interactive cable, from communications satellites to word processors, from voice activated systems to electronic environmental sensors.

Summary. Computer assisted techniques will be routine and essential to all planning and data handling. They should not be a subject of primary concern in starting an issues management program.

Technique: Small Group Processes

So much of issues management involves meetings with small groups (2 to 50 people) who frequently have not met before, come from different backgrounds, who are uncertain about the purpose and value of what they are becoming involved with, and have different behavior patterns in group meetings, that close attention must be given to how those meetings are handled. Closely related to the small group process is the mechanism for the delivery of information to successively higher echelons in the organization. Well known, but often ignored, is that the higher one goes in an organization, the less likely that person is to be able or willing to read an extended treatise and the more accustomed he or she is to oral communication.

From another point of view, things do not just happen. An environment and a process must be set in place by the issues manager or issues coordinator to make things happen in a way that is effective, creative, salient to the issue, the organization, and individual interest, and effective in structuring the next step toward decision-making, the assignment of responsibilities and action.

Techniques are available for doing this; some are discussed elsewhere in this document, including the conversational Delphi, the Consensor, executive panels, networks, and purchase and rental services. The sense of the small group process permeates those techniques discussed in this section.

The keys to a successful meeting include the following:

- People should know why they are there.

- They should know the purpose of the meeting.

- They should know what is expected of them.

- The processes should make it natural for everyone to have a turn to speak, without rigidly forcing participation.

- At the early stage of meetings intended to be creative or generative, critical comments should be held to a minimum. Evaluation, sorting, and critique is often best separated from idea generation and done either later at the same meeting or at a different time. This rule is well-known and well documented in the principles of brainstorming.

Other techniques to assure that each person is heard involve various forms of a round robin. Each person, in turn, is asked to respond to the same question. Only after everyone has responded does one get to the discussion and further evaluation. A formal process for running round robins is available under the title, "Nominal Group Technique."

It is often desirable to experiment with new methods and techniques with a group which is forgiving, interested, and willing to try. Under no circumstances try a method or technique with senior managers that you have not repeatedly used and have full mastery of.

In terms of learning small group processes, there are texts and guides; opportunities at meetings to experience them; and consultant services to teach these techniques.

To give the reader a sense that this area of small group processes does have a bag of tricks that are well recognized, here is a list of some of the techniques which are effective and can be taught:

- Brainwriting (ideawriting).

- Brainstorming.

- Charrette.

- Nominal group technique.

- Interpretive structural modeling.

- Generation of causal loop diagrams, consequence diagrams, or signed digraphs.

- Gaming.

- Mock processes, such as mock hearings.

- Policy capturing.

- Role playing.

- Videotape of role playing.

- KSIM and QSIM (computer assisted systems dynamic models usable in small groups).

- The conference telephone call.

- Picturephone conference.

Recommendation. Try on several for fit and comfort.

Technique: Scenario Building

Scenarios are a widely used tool in corporate and organizational planning. Taking the basic definition of Kahn and Wiener from their 1967 book, *The Year 2000, A Framework for Speculation on the Next Thirty-Three Years*, a scenario is "a hypothetical sequence of events constructed for the purpose of focusing attention on causal processes and decision points." A more up-to-the-minute definition reflecting current practice is put forward by Warfield and his associates, "A scenario is a narrative description of a possible state of affairs or development over time. It can be very useful to communicate speculative thoughts about future developments, to elicit discussion and feedback, and to stimulate the imagination. Scenarios generally are based on qualitative expert information, but may include quantitative information as well."

The scenario is a technique to deal with a core problem of a study of the future. The individual trends do not automatically come together to create useful images of the future applicable to planning. A primary purpose of the scenario is to create these holistic, integrated images of how the future may evolve. Those images, in turn, become the context for planning, a testbed for ideas, or the stimulus for new development.

Reflecting the corporate practice at General Electric, Ian Wilson notes the following objectives in G.E.'s use of scenarios:

1. To combine alternate environmental developments into a framework which is relatively consistent and relevant to the future of the company.

2. To identify "branching points," potential discontinuities and contingencies which will serve as early warning systems, and for which contingency plans can be prepared.

3. To formulate a framework which makes it possible to translate alternative environmental developments into economic terms and alternate economic forecasts. (In effect, the scenarios served as the basis for the long-range economic forecasts.)

4. To provide the basis for analyzing the range of possible outcomes which result from the interaction between alternate environments and:

   —Variable industry/market growth.

   —Company operating results on current trajectories, thus seeing how the Company as a whole (with its mix of products and services) responds to these consistent futures.

5. To test the outcomes of various Company and competitor strategies in alternate environments.

Figure 3-4 shows the generic process for the construction of scenarios.

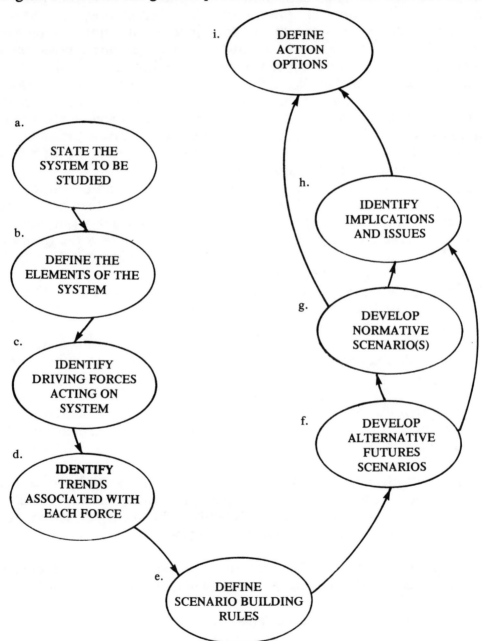

Figure 3-4. Scenario Building for Policy Use

Source: J.F. Coates, Inc.

Experience shows that a critical problem is the proper number of scenarios. There can be an infinite number, exceeding any practical use, or one can make the equally serious error of choosing a best or most likely scenario. The concept underlying these scenarios is that the future is only partially formed, hence there are many real possibilities which must be explored. Usually a minimum of three scenarios and rarely more than five are used in a policy process. In Figure 3-4 the key step, in defining the rules for building a scenario, in part determines the number of scenarios that will be effective. It should be notes that, if in Figure 3-4 one goes merely from "f" to "h," and on to "j," one is dealing only with response and coping situations. It is essential to go through stage "g," the development of desired, normative, or sought-for futures. This emphasizes the positive and creative side of futures planning and scenario building.

Again drawing on the General Electric work, Figure 3-5 shows two qualitative scenarios and Figure 3-6 summarizes four scenarios in a skeletal format.

The use of scenarios in a more current context is that, for example, of ALCOA, where a group of scenarios was developed and legitimated through a series of internal workshops. The product was then delivered to various business units to be used as background in the development of their particular strategic plans.

The key problem in the use of scenarios in planning flows from the mix of qualitative and quantitative factors, and the inevitable range of alternatives. The planning difficulty is drawing the implications for planning from the full range of scenarios; in other words, avoiding choosing a preferred or a most likely image of the future.

There is no formal way of dealing with that difficulty. Continual feedback and interaction seems to be the only method at the moment which works.

The literature on scenarios is quite extensive and can lead in several directions; in some places, it can lead to role playing as a way of understanding developments. At one extreme, it can result in wargaming and at the trivial level it can give one almost useless four-cell matrices of the development of two variables. In general, one wants and can use mixed qualitative and quantitative inputs for a complex, holistic image of alternative futures.

Summary. The use of scenarios is widely practiced and generally favorably endorsed by those who use them. They present substantial conceptual barriers for those first moving into their application. Some of the difficulties are associated with the fact that virtually any futures technique can be used as input, quantitative to totally qualitative, and that their employment involves an element of play, which is uncommon in large organizations.

TWO SCENARIOS ON THE FUTURE OF BUSINESS *

On the theory that future outcomes can, to some extent, be shaped by constructive, anticipatory action, this pair of scenarios was developed in 1973 (as part of a set of four) to illustrate the differences that might flow from divergent business responses to the emerging "qualitative expectations" of the post-WW II generation in the United States.

SCENARIO OF A REACTIVE BUSINESS RESPONSE

"Beset by inflation, recession, shortages and a profit squeeze, and confronted by the recent spate of newly-legislative requirements (e.g., EEO, OSHA, product safety, pollution control), business opts for a policy of 'minimum feasible compliance.' Having no realistic option but to comply with the law, companies attempt to deal with the 'revolution of qualitative expectations' simply by adhering to the minimum requirements of new statutes. They challenge administrative interpretations of the law whenever possible, and resist pressures for new legislation wherever they develop.

"For a while the public, distracted by concern over rising prices, unemployment, and declining incomes, and disillusioned and distrustful in the post-Watergate climate, is content to see the assimilation and enforcement of 1970-1973 legislation. Meanwhile, however, the basic forces working toward a further shift in societal values continue to work their way through society, and a 'business-as-usual' attitude on the part of companies does little or nothing to deal with the developing challenge.

"The advent of the political year 1976, and the emergence of a younger, better educated and more aggressive work force and electorate set the stage for a new round of anti-business legislation. In particular, the perceived failure of business to deal adequately with the conflicting claims of the energy crisis and a clean environment leads to the introduction of bills, and the writing of planks in party platforms, to control business growth and investment, and to restructure major industries. A change of Administration and continued business 'heel-dragging' ensure passage of many of these bills by 1978.

"At the same time, a basic inability to deal with the 'quality of work' expectations of the new work force leads to progressively declining morale and productivity, increasing unionization, alienation and 'whistle-blowing.' Business, suffering a crisis of confidence and failure of nerve, is by now in a virtual state of siege, harassed by government regulation, beset by boycotts and class-action suits, 'betrayed' by its employees, and obsessed with a 'fortress mentality.' All that remains is the final step of public control and take-over of major corporations."

* See Wilson in J. Fowles, *Handbook of Futures Research*, pp. 236-37.

Figure 3-5. Two Scenarios on the Future of Business

SCENARIO OF A PRO-ACTIVE BUSINESS RESPONSE

"Compliance with both the letter and the spirit of current laws, and the sponsorship of new legislation and public information programs, are only starting points in this strategy. These efforts are buttressed by the establishment and enforcement of standards and self-policing activities on such matters as advertising, consumer rights and product safety.

"The major emphasis, however, is not on the legislative/educative aspects, but rather on innovative approaches to corporate marketing, production and management policies that, over the next decade, lead to a sweeping reform of business relations with customers, employees, government and the public. The need for thorough-going revisions of many conventional methods and policies flows from an awareness that, in many instances (such as pollution abatement, conservation of energy/materials, product servicing, job re-structuring), a 'tinkering' or 'additive' approach is not only less effective, but also more costly in the long run.

"Progress, inevitably, is slow because of institutional inertia, costs and conflicting claims on management attention. But it is sufficiently noticeable that the gap between expectations and performance is kept manageable and tension does not reach the breaking-point. Although corporate mistakes occur, and are well publicized, the public attitude toward them is marked by a greater degree of tolerance than in other scenarios. Penalties are imposed more selectively, and Congress is less apt to reach for 'shotgun' legislation. Such laws as are passed tend to embody and codify the best of current business practices.

"The value of a pro-active response becomes apparent, too, in the work force area. As the changing composition and wants/needs of the labor force reach critical levels in the latter half of the decade, the early experiments in job enlargement/flexible scheduling/participation start to pay rich dividends in enabling companies to attract and retain a committed and productive work force.

"Pressure from consumer, environmental and other interest groups continues to be a major factor, but a great openness in corporate communications (including more voluntary disclosure of corporate information) keeps this pressure at a low level of acrimony. In general, while there may be greater 'publicization' of the corporation than there was in 1970, there is markedly less 'politicization' of economic decision-making than in the other scenarios."

Figure 3-5. Two Scenarios on the Future of Business (Continued)

SCENARIO I Benchmark Probability: 50%	SCENARIO II More Inward-Looking Societies (Current Trajectory) Probability: 25%	SCENARIO III More Integrated Societies Probability: 15%	SCENARIO IV More Disarrayed Societies Probability: 10%
International Reduced threats of large-scale military conflicts, but level of U.S.-Communist world tension continues	General preoccupation with national interests, and low level of conflict (though potential for future conflict remains). Relative stability as result of domestic preoccupations, political diffidence, or ideological decline	Relatively peaceful, relatively prosperous, relatively arms-controlled world. Flareups which spill over borders are closely policed	Unstable world as result of conflicting national interests or renewed ideological influence
Emergence of multipolar system, U.S.-USSR-EEC-Japan: More regional groupings elsewhere	Same as I, except less progress in regional groupings	Relatively high degree of consultation among nations, and political coordination (even integration) among most nations	Fluctuations between multi-polar power distribution and renewed world bipolarity
"Nixon Doctrine" of lower U.S. profile reduces direct involvement but steps up aid (including multilateral aid)	U.S. cuts its foreign involvement and avoids military intervention: aid chiefly designed to support trading system	Ambitious multilateral development projects are successful; progress on population control	U.S. meets stark, aggressive provocations and challenges to presumed spheres of influence
Third World continues troubled by regional/local conflicts and by internal revolutionary movements	Same as I, except more internal revolutions	Visible development progress; North-South Gap perceived as narrowing	Third World is disrupted by extreme and internal upheaval; many radical insurrections and economic breakdowns with famines
World trade continues to rise at about 10-11% a year	Slow growth of world trade, 6-8% annual increase	Growth of world trade (including East-West trade) at about 12-15% a year	World trade level is maintained out of necessity
U.S. share of world exports continues to decline; U.S. industrial imports rise faster than exports, and BOP difficulties continue	Sharper decline of U.S. share of world trade than in I; increased protectionism	Export of high technology equipment and services produces balance in BOP; offshore manufacturing and imports of labor-intensive products are encouraged	Dollar under pressure, with valuation a high probability; offshore investment declines sharply

* See Wilson in J. Fowles, *Handbook of Futures Research*, pp. 244-45.

Figure 3-6. Summary of Four Alternative Scenarios, 1971-1980

SCENARIO I Benchmark Probability: 50%	SCENARIO II More Inward-Looking Societies (Current Trajectory) Probability: 25%	SCENARIO III More Integrated Societies Probability: 15%	SCENARIO IV More Disarrayed Societies Probability: 10%
Domestic (U.S.) Increased demand for, but limited progress on, "new priorities" (environment, housing, education, medical care); Increasing levels of "mainstream America" frustration, continuing protest but less violent	Roughly same as I, but less progress on new priorities; more polarization and protests	Visible and real progress on new priorities; new political will; fear of crisis overcome	Deep fear of crisis, gradual erosion of political will; deep divisions; breakdown of infra-structure; new priority is defense
Business response to new priorities slow because of market mechanisms; but increasing government-business partnerships	Business influence declines; curtailment of multinational corporations, offshore production; increased unionization	Effective business response to consumerism and environ-mental problems; dynamic involvement in housing, urban renewal, new communities; improved public image of business	Stagnation of private sector; decline in R&D
Slow trend toward humanizing institutions; groping for new participative mechanisms	Increased bureaucratization; hard line on deviations from norm (crime, drugs, etc.)	More consensus, sense of progress; increased involve-ment of minorities and youth in decision-making on community level	Mood of fear, control, and repression
Slight shift in work/leisure balance toward latter	Hours of work stays on current trajectory	Longer vacations, more holidays and sabbaticals are the norm	Average work week longer than in I, II, and III; but 10% of manhours lost due to strikes
Government influence increasing over business and people's lives	Political swing to right; attempt to legislate solutions	"New Federalism" extends to business and other private organizations	Large-scale government bureaucracies and control
Government expenditures rise as % of GNP; defense budget declines through 1972, then levels off	Tax revolts hold down government revenues, spending; defense budget slightly higher than in I.	Increased government spending on new priorities (result of peace dividend, U.S.-USSR detente); defense budget stabilizes in absolute terms	Defense spending high for omnidirectional defense; large government deficits
Relatively high level of unemployment (c. 4%)	Higher level of unemployment	Low unemployment	High unemployment
Productivity growth rate, c. 3% per annum; some improvement in services	Productivity continues on current (1965-1969) trajectory	Higher productivity; significant improvement in services	Low level of productivity
Relatively high level of inflation (c. 3%)	Higher level of inflation (c. 4%)	Lower level of inflation (c. 2%)	Potential runaway inflation (c. 6%)

Figure 3-6. Summary of Four Alternative Scenarios, 1971-1980

Technique: Incidental Techniques of Some Use in Issues Management

The following tools have been reported in one or more places as applicable to issues management. They cropped up in our interviews. We note them because they have apparently found a place in at least one organization's activities and may trigger off useful applications in others.

- *Economic analysis.* Economic analysis is obviously a central factor in long-range planning of capital investments. The particular value in issues management is in issues identification. A rough cut evaluation of the cost of the alternative ways in which an emerging issue may be resolved is a valuable tool in two ways:

  —It helps set priorities for an issue in relation to other issues.

  —It gives some hints as to the range of costs of alternative outcomes of an issue.

- *Key player analysis* is something of a catch phrase, which does not involve any particular formal process. As employed by more experienced organizations, it refers to the identification of who the various actors will be in the unfolding policy process, and among those various actors, which ones will exercise critical or key influence. Key player analysis is particularly useful in dealing with Congressional or State House analyses of an emerging legislative issue. It permits one to identify various members and committees in terms of their responsibilities and concerns and the interest groups likely to impinge on those players. This, in turn, permits one to target monitoring and actions.

- *Trend extrapolation.* We have found relatively little interest in formal trend extrapolations of the sort generally implied by technological forecasting and market research. Trend extrapolation, however, is a potentially powerful technique when coupled to an issues identification program and an interactive computer software package, the value there being that it will permit a trend to be established by whatever means an organization normally establishes trends. Then a group of senior managers, executive planners, or staff people can play with "what if" assumptions with regard to alternative developments and their influence on those trends.

- *Identification of possible trigger events.* This is another catch phrase for an unspecified activity. Any good issues management team looks for events that would gel wide concern or trigger a new response. There is, however, no formal process for doing this. It is a combination of wit, wisdom, experience, and close and careful speculative attention. The search for triggers may influence the tracking program.

- *Issues modeling.* Issues modeling is another catch phrase which has no specific meaning, but refers to the comprehensive defining of all the aspects of an issue including the actors, the policy options, the choices, mutual alternative developments, and options for industry, for other actors, and for the company. It is virtually equivalent to all the things that go into understanding an issue.

Technique: Techniques Not in General Use

A number of techniques applicable to technological forecasting or the formal aspects of strategic planning and to detailed budgetary analysis have potential applications in a complex issues management program, but we have found no evidence of their use. This lack of use in an issues management program does not imply that the techniques are not appropriate for strategic planning:

- *Correlation and regression*, as the formal mathematical process.

- *Decision analysis* and the reciprocal process of *policy capturing* and the use of judgment theory have not been noted in any of the literature or the interviews.

- *Sensitivity analysis* has not been used in the formal sense, which implies a mathematically structured model in which one measures the implications of changes in certain variables. Sensitivity analysis is a variation on parametric analysis, a technique which we also have not found used, except in the techniques described elsewhere under Decision Support Systems and spreadsheet analysis.

- *Factor analysis*, like regression techniques, is another neglected but potentially important tool in issues management. It should, for example, be practical with a large enough database in hand to factor analyze the state or local considerations entering into the adoption of a new regulation, constraint, ruling, or technology. Obviously, such a move to quantitation would be interesting in adding a new level of sophistication to qualitative judgment and to key player analysis.

4

ESTABLISHING AN ISSUES MANAGEMENT SYSTEM

INTRODUCTION

This section draws together the organizational experience and the analysis of methods and techniques described in other sections to present a generic description of a typical, effective issues management system within a large organization. The generic description is not intended to be a recommendation but only initial guidance for those who would consider establishing an issues management system.

For those who would seek information and assistance beyond this text and references there are several associations which have a specific interest in issues management, such as The Conference Board, the National Association of Manufacturers, and the Issues Management Association.

Issues management systems in industry and trade associations, as noted earlier, tend to settle into one of three organizational locations: public relations, strategic planning, or policy analysis units. In successful issues management programs, however, there should be active, broad participation by most if not all units of the organization and an effective communication channel to the executive committee and the CEO. The system could be located in a strategic planning unit, or distributed more broadly across divisions; ultimately it should involve the active participation of all units.

A comprehensive program must deal with both long-term implications for the organization, five, ten or more years in the future, and with the intermediate implications two to five years ahead. Issues management must also relate long-range issues to more immediate, pressing problems and opportunities. The defining theme is the long-term interests of the organization, not short-term fire fighting.

An incremental approach, starting modestly and learning by doing, is most appropriate. An initial, conservative, relatively spartan, low profile system with success to its credit should evolve into a more elaborate, sophisticated, and useful system.

In general, it is risky to jump into issues identification and management as a full-blown, highly capitalized and staffed operation, since this could involve a significant change in organizational structures or communication channels and hence disrupt established ways. Close attention should go into nurturing a system and process that fits the organization and meets its needs.

This takes sensitivity and skill, and intimate knowledge of the organization on the part of those who are fostering and encouraging the development of the issues management services.

The generic model of issues management described below, if implemented, would assist and support all these objectives.

THE PROTOTYPICAL SYSTEM

Step 1 - Diagnosis

Decide whether issues identification and management makes sense for your organization.

In the last few years, have there been unanticipated problems coming from factors outside the organization that repeatedly resulted in unmet objectives, that disappointed reasonable expectations, or that forced unwelcome changes in the organization's operating procedures? Looking back, can you identify points when foreknowledge of what was coming, or a better understanding of what was happening, would have pointed to a more desirable management strategy than the one you used? Looking forward, are there uncertainties about the immediate and mid-term future that impinge on current decision-making? If so, an issues management process is indicated.

Would the operating managers welcome pertinent information about developing trends and emerging problems, even if it widened the company's options and raised questions about the wisdom of current operating practices? If so, an issues management process may be workable.

Would your managers see an early warning system as a questioning of their competence and a threat to their authority? If so, an issues management process may be difficult to introduce, even if it is needed.

A low profile, low cost, "experimental" beginning that is tactfully introduced, managed by trusted insiders, and easy to walk away from should it not work, is the most promising solution to this situation.

Step 2 - Begin Small

Begin with a process that can be hand-tailored by a proven, innovative manager to fit the organization's decision-making process and its needs, and that can evolve and grow if it proves useful.

Give the experiment the commitment and the resources (which will not be large) that it needs to succeed, but treat it as an earnest experiment which can be concluded if it does not work, without a disaster to the career of a valued member of the staff.

Establish a small issues management working group or team with instructions to:

1. Start an issues identification system based on literature scanning.

2. Systematically develop and test simple analytical tools and information delivery modes and mechanisms of issues identification.

In the beginning. Appoint an issues manager or issues coordinator.

- He or she should be intimately familiar with the organization, the industry, the workings of any advisory structure, the decision-making process, the distribution of authority and responsibility within the organization, and the effective channels of communication already in use.

Establish a small *ad hoc* issues management team, chosen from across all organizational elements.

- The *ad hoc* team members will devote only a portion of their time to these activities at this point, and are not full-time staff for this project or office. As the issues coordinator develops the system the members of the *ad hoc* team may either join the staff or become members of the issues management committee.

Begin scanning activity, as described below.

Develop products, systematic procedures, structure and staff slowly and in parallel. Anticipate having a system approximating that described below within two to three years.

Organization. The issues coordinator, selected from within the management structure, may or may not start with a small professional staff.

The *ad hoc* issues management team should evolve into an issues management committee, made up of personnel from all divisions of the organization, meeting regularly to fulfill specific responsibilities.

Products and Services. Products and services of the team may include:

- Regularly issued briefs, possibly in the form of a newsletter, identifying and describing trends and issues of interest to the organization or to specific divisions, which may have an impact on the organization directly or on its clients, customers, workers, etc.

- Backgrounders, or summary papers—which will be updated as appropriate—on the more important issues as they evolve and change.

- Alerts to appropriate levels of management, if an issue appears likely to become suddenly more important, threatening, or actionable.

- Fully developed analyses of issues, as they become of active interest to management, with a range of action options if so requested.

- Combining service, organization, and procedural functions, there must be provision for access to the most senior managers. This usually means access to the executive committee on a periodic or as appropriate basis.

Procedures. As a first step the issues coordinator, with the help of the *ad hoc* team and suggestions solicited from others, should draw up a list of 50-100 publications to be scanned:

- Include (1) all of those generally relied on for information about the industry, government policy and regulations; (2) general news magazines and national and regional newspapers, (3) a representative sample of interdisciplinary, scientific and engineering journals, making sure to include journals of economic, social, and behavioral sciences; (4) business-oriented magazines; (5) science-oriented popular magazines; (6) environmental and other issue-oriented periodicals; (7) a sampling of trade journals (construction, services, appliance manufacturers, recreation, and other appropriate industries); (8) journals of political criticism and political advocacy.

Establish scanning teams by soliciting volunteers from all technical, marketing, public information staff and operating divisions. Assign each member to scan one or two periodicals regularly and systematically. Do this by mutual agreement—that is, let team members pick what they want to read, or do read anyway.

Provide members of the scanning team with (a) a brief explanation of objectives and guidelines, (b) examples of the kinds of things they should scan for, (c) a beginning set of topics to scan for, and (d) blank scanning and tracking forms (see example, Figures 2-6 and 2-7).

Have the issues coordinator and the issues management committee review scanning and tracking topics at least twice yearly.

The issues coordinator and committee should also establish and periodically update a shorter list of "tracking subjects" to be given high priority and attention.

Instruct scanning team members to regularly scan assigned periodicals, and sources selected by choice or come upon accidentally, for news and information directly or indirectly related to the tracking and scanning topics, or which suggest topics that should be considered for the list.

Scanners will collect items by copying, abstracting, or noting a citation, and send them to the issues management team or manager.

The issues coordinator and any staff will review, abstract, collate, integrate, and interpret this material and present it to the issues management committee for further evaluation.

Using aids like the matrices shown in Figure 4-1, the committee will evaluate the material and sort it into categories, for example, "immediate and urgent," "tracking and monitoring," or "no action."

This particular stage of the operation can vary widely, depending on the number and rank of the people involved, time available from the issues management committee, and the staff support available to the issues coordinator. In some good practices, the review and interpretation of the material is a function of the issues management committee and in other organizations, some prefabricated material is presented to them by the issues coordinator.

The committee may instruct the issues coordinator to prepare a brief on important issues. He or she may use several resources in carrying out this task: internal staff only, consultants, workshops, etc.

The issues coordinator at regular intervals will prepare newsletters or other delivery formats to keep the organization management and staff aware of developing and emerging issues.

The issues coordinator and committee should jointly determine when it is appropriate to issue alerts or offer presentations and to what level of management, if an issue becomes significantly more important or more urgent.

Decisions and actions in response to an issue will be determined by management and assigned to personnel at the appropriate level for implementation, with the issues coordinator and his committee serving as information resources and advisors, as requested.

External Support. The issues coordinator should establish an external network of contact with issues managers in other companies, associations, and professional societies, by no means limited to the organization's primary industrial sector but cutting across many business and industrial activities. Strengthening linkages to others helps in identifying and interpreting emerging trends and developments.

The issues coordinator may be provided with small resources for the purchase of outside services, such as tracking of state, multi-state, or national legislative and regulatory actions, and for commercial news, clipping, and monitoring services to expand and complement the internal coverage.

Figure 4-2 is a model of the elements of the issues management process as it may evolve.

Two preliminary evaluation matrices are shown.

(1)
      Consider issues A, B, C, D and E. How important is each one, on a scale
of 1 to 10, to the company? The average score by the rating group for each
issue is given in column 1 in the tabulation below.
      What is the probability, on a scale of 0.0 to 1.0, that this issue or event
will come to pass by the end of 1980? The average score for each issue
appears in column 2.
      What is the product of impact and probability for each issue? (See
column 3.)

Issue	1 *Impact* *(1-10)*	2 *Probability of* *Occurrence* *(0.0-1.0)*	3 *Impact x* *Probability*	4 *Ranking* *of Issue*
A	8.8	0.3	2.64	4
B	6.7	0.7	4.69	1
C	4.4	0.9	3.96	2
D	3.8	0.8	3.04	3
E	2.1	0.5	1.05	5

(2) **Impact and Probability of Occurrence Matrix**

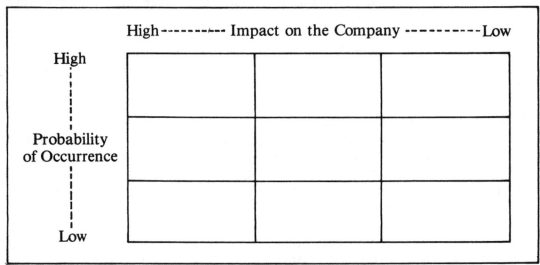

Figure 4-1. Two Evaluation Matrices

Source: James K. Brown, *This Business of Issues: Coping
        with the Company's Environment*, The Conference
        Board, New York, 1980, pp. 31-2.

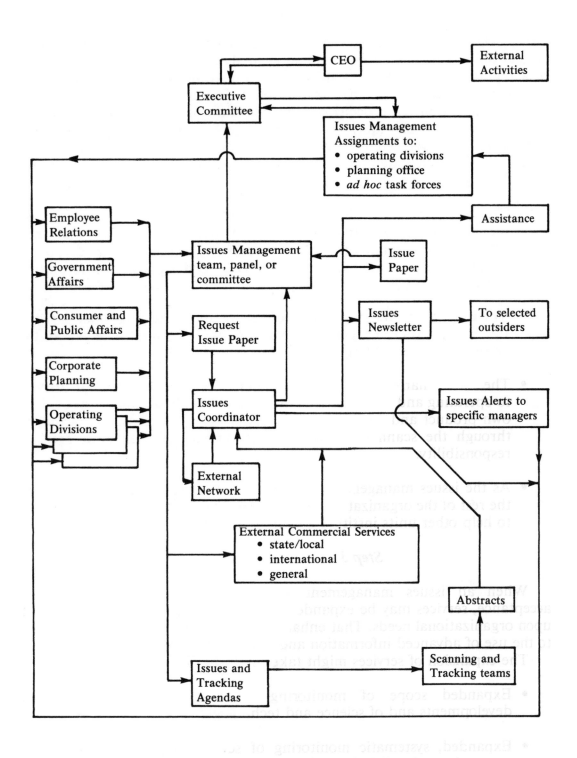

Figure 4-2. An Issues Management Process

Issues Management in Organizational Sub-Units. In many organizations, special units—such as an environmental analysis unit, a public affairs unit, or a regulatory analysis unit—may wish to institute an issues management system in the absence of an organization-wide interest or commitment. In some organizations, the decision may be made to experiment with issues management in one unit, as a prototype or model for subsequent consideration by the parent organization.

Successful issues identification and management in a sub-unit requires several things:

- The special focus should not unduly narrow the scope of scanning and monitoring; for example, scanning for trends and issues that may affect the environment should encompass a wide range of social, demographic, economic, technological, and political information sources.

- The process should emphasize describing and analyzing links between the trend, event, or potential change and potential effects on the special focus of concern.

- The issues management group or team should build informal bridges to operating and other service units, both to build appreciation of their own product and to have a channel for information that is acquired through the scanning process but is outside of their own area of responsibility.

- As the issues management procedures are developed and are seen by the rest of the organization to work well, the group should be prepared to help other units institute a similar process.

Step 3 - Gradual Expansion

When an issues management system is established and there is acceptance, services may be expanded and capabilities enhanced depending upon organizational needs. That enhanced service may give special emphasis to the use of advanced information and telecommunications technologies.

The expansion of services might take the form of:

- Expanded scope of monitoring of political and international developments and of science and technology.

- Expanded, systematic monitoring of selected environmental, social, economic, and political trend areas that are often precursors of major societal events and changes.

- Joint ventures with other organizations to probe and explore issues of common interest, to test and evaluate methods and techniques and to exchange knowledge and experience.

- Increased use of computer assisted activities to enhance capabilities. This might for example take the form of:

  —Computerization of issues management databases and expanded capability to access and use external databases.

  —Extensive use of computer-assisted analysis or modeling.

  —Formation of an electronic network of communications.

  —Test and evaluation of analytical and impact analysis programs such as QUEST, INTERAX, KSIM, LEAP, and various Delphi programs, for application to the organization's problems.

Making it all Work

The issues coordinator or issues manager as the linchpin of the operation would be well advised to heed the practical advice from other issues managers, summarized in Chapter 3. The vital points are:

- Be positive

- Be helpful

- Be informed

- Be a team player

- Be interdisciplinary

- Be sensitive to the culture

- Be active in outreach

- Be selective

- Be smart

5

A RESEARCH AGENDA

Throughout preceding chapters, we have identified areas and issues of uncertainty. These can comprise a checklist of topics for experimentation and research to add to the knowledge and guidance base for initiating and conducting an issues management program.

To explore further the need for research and to identify more specifically the targets for a research agenda, J.F. Coates, Inc. conducted two workshops in July/August 1985 on "Issues Identification and Management: Developing a Research Agenda." They were sponsored by the Electric Power Research Institute.

Workshop participants came from the universities, the electric utility industry, government, trade associations, consultants, vendors of scanning and survey services, and corporations.

In preparation, invitees were asked in a telephone interview if, (a) they believed there are researchable questions that can be asked about issues management: (b) if so, what were they, and (c) are there areas which if addressed systematically by research, would make more effective the operation of an issues management program? Fifty-two research topics were suggested in ninety interviews.

The two workshops were designed around exercises and discussions in which the participants would work as individuals and in groups to develop an agenda for issues management research.

Participants worked in groups to develop models of the issues management process. There was general agreement on the issues management process within an organization although there were a number of differences, especially over the meaning of terms such as "issues management." The purpose of modeling issues management was to ensure that participants had a clear image of the scope of the process to be considered later for the research agenda. Their instructions were to describe the process from the earliest glimmer of an issue to final closeout on that issue.

Participants were asked to tell of instances of success and failure of issues management in which they had been involved. These case histories provided a perspective of what participants considered good issues management.

With this information and their generic process model as a base, the participants returned to their working groups to draw up a list of topics for research. They were asked to pay attention to the ideal outcomes and benefits for the issues management process of such research; to consider who would sponsor it; who would do it, in what length of time and for what size budget. The lists of research topics reported back to the meeting were assembled and rank ordered by group vote.

THE ROLE OF RESEARCH IN ISSUES MANAGEMENT

Research on issues management will have a variety of independent outcomes. In the near term research may support and legitimate existing issues managers, their programs and processes. For the issues manager, research may serve to discharge some uncertainties, as well as raising new questions. A growing body of research will bring new theories, new concepts, new, and improved, tools and technologies.

Beyond these outcomes, however, there are suggestions that research which improves the issues management process and professionalizes the issues manager may also improve the effectiveness of organizations, and develop issues management as a new paradigm of management, and a potentially positive social and political force.

The following are suggested as five clusters of positive outcomes of research:

Support for Existing Programs of Issues Management

- Supporting existing programs and individuals.

- Legitimating the enterprise.

- Supporting action.

- Providing better training for issues managers.

- Improving the effectiveness of small resources.

New Methodologies

- Breakthroughs in analysis and methodology.

- Refining tools and methods; a new bag of tools.

  —Better identification of issues, ranking, and consensus formation.

  —Predictive models of issues development.

  —Better understanding of non-predictive models; of the uncertainty factor of models and how to deal with uncertainty.

New Theories and Concepts

- The development of a theory of issues management that would display the underlying causes of issues.

- Moving from operating at a primitive level to being able to foresee impacts and act intelligently at a higher level.

- Acting as a semi-objective early warning system.

- Enabling the formulation of valid conclusions on specific issues.

Improved Organizational Effectiveness

- Concluding that techniques already exist which top management can use to make better decisions.

- Increasing the awareness among top management of the social impacts of their business decisions.

- Increasing the autonomy of a corporation, its ability to be in control of its own destiny.

- Alternatively, improving a corporation's management of its interdependent relationships with others and with other organizations.

- Increasing profits.

- Improving coordination at earlier stages for focused industry-wide approaches.

- Providing the ordinary worker with the ability to assess issues affecting his or her organization.

More Effective Action

- Making a positive response from industry more credible and more likely.

- Dramatically improving organizational and national productivity.

- (Issues management) acting as a credible positive force in the political sector.

- Giving greater confidence in the system and in the nation as a whole.

THE PRIORITIES FOR RESEARCH

After generating topics for a research agenda, discussing and sorting them, the following five items were ranked highest in importance by participants of both workshops. A number of topics suggested by participants overlapped or covered similar ground. These have been combined or grouped together.

1. Early warning signals—what and where are the origins of an issue? What is the underlying trend?

2. Methods and techniques of issues management, especially the most effective and economic means of environmental scanning and screening.

3. How do you measure or evaluate success? What are the criteria? Does a formal, intentional, issues management program make a difference? What can be learned from case studies? What can cost-benefit analysis tell us?

4. The role of outside perspectives in issues management, for example, those of stockholders, customers, experts, and government.

5. Modeling issues management—concepts, implementation, validation, testing, evaluation,

   —predictive models

   —computers and expert systems

Other high priority topics for research: these received at least two votes when the list of research topics was rank ordered.

6. Pretesting and evaluation of strategies for action and intervention using tools from other fields, marketing, for example.

7. How close to corporate leadership does issues management stand? Can decision-makers learn to take risks in issues management and survive?

   —The extent of corporate awareness and use of issues management.

   —To what extent is issues management likely to change managerial practice?

   —The relationship of crisis management and issues management.

—Corporate social responsibility in issues management.

—The definition of an issue in organizational terms.

8. The typology of issues, issue lifecycles.

9. How could our concept of accounting, of measurement and reward be altered to include a perspective of future value and long-term contribution?

10. How to get the unthinkable on the table.

11. Internal issue development techniques.

Many other research topics were generated by the workshop participants. The entire list is given in Table 5-1.

In pre-meeting interviews, 52 topics for research were suggested. Many of these topics are similar to those suggested by the workshop participants. The interviewees' top five priorities were:

1. Where should the organization locate the issues management function?

2. What can be learned from case studies? The use of case material to acquire knowledge and build understanding.

3. How do you "sell" issues management to top managers?

   —How do you get their attention?

   —How can you understand and anticipate their perspectives?

   —How does issues management relate to the mentality of different managers?

   —How does issues management relate to the power structure within the organization?

4. How does the structure of the firm relate to successful issues management?

5. The definition of issues management.

For a more extensive list of topics from these interviews, see Table 5-2.

WHO BENEFITS FROM ISSUES MANAGEMENT RESEARCH

Successful issues management is likely to produce benefits for the practitioner and the issues manager, and probably also for:

- Decision-makers, who as prime actors, will be more informed and supported in their strategic choices.

- Other users of issues management such as planners, civil servants, trade associations, governmental affairs officials, who will gain better public policy decisions.

- Academics and students will benefit from an improved curriculum and new theoretical understanding.

- Consumers, adversaries, the public, will gain from recognition of the value of their perspective on issues.

WHO SHOULD FUND THE RESEARCH

Business-oriented sources, such as corporations, trade associations, and professional groups are the most likely sources of funding for research, for example, the Conference Board, EPRI, the Public Relations Society of America.
Other possible sources, especially for university research, are the National Science Foundation, other federal agencies and state government.

WHO ARE THE RESEARCHERS

Academics and consultants are the most likely choice to do issues management research, provided they are willing to be results oriented, familiar with business approaches and have practical experience in the field.

OBSERVATIONS AND COMMENTS ON THE RESEARCH AGENDA

Participants commented on the research agenda. A number of individual observations and dissenting views are noted here and these include some reviewers' comments.

- The agenda reflects a greater interest in scanning and screening methods than research on outcomes of this process, which is surprising, considering the number of scanning services available and the likelihood that senior managers will be more interested in the potential opportunity or threat revealed by the process.

- What is at issue is the most economic, efficient and effective means of scanning, from the point of view of how issues managers spend time.

- Research into issues management divides into two categories: (1) theoretical, which includes concepts of models, their implementation, validation and testing, and (2) practical, including methods, techniques, and tactics, and a better understanding of influence points, which can be used for intervention.

- A distinction must be made between research on issues and interest in the specifics of an individual issue, and issues management research, which looks at the process of identifying and managing those issues.

- Involving adversaries in the issues management process is an important aspect of monitoring the external environment in order to be aware of the direction they see the issue moving.

- Identifying stakeholders may be useful in relating the value of issues management to decision-makers.

- The exploration of alternative methods of working with stakeholders may be fruitful.

- How might the practice of issues management be seen by external interest groups? Their sense might be that issues management is being developed in order to undercut the democratic process. One possible answer may be to professionalize the occupation of issues manager and to encourage more participation by outside groups in the practice of issues management.

- Activist interest groups have been effective managers of their issues. There are lessons to be learned from their work.

- The links between issues management and political strategies are important in developing an action orientation. Are certain political strategies more appropriate and effective at different stages of an issue's lifecycle? An investigation would be useful.

- The potential as well as actual links between issues management and strategic planning ought to be explored. One important aspect is time—how long is an organization's response time on an issue? How long does it take an issue to work through an organization and can that time be shortened?

CONCLUDING OBSERVATIONS AND COMMENTS

Participants were asked for their suggestions for next steps and their observations and comments on the workshops. The following summarizes their comments and those of reviewers.

Issues management can be characterized as an emerging discipline still tentative on its place in the organizational hierarchy and seeking consensus on methods and techniques of operation. Its history in some ways parallels that of other managerial tools such as operations research and futures research, implying that there are crossover lessons from these disciplines. The map of research topics in futures research developed in 1977 by Wayne Boucher might, for example, be laid over the agenda for issues management research and examined for similarities.

A radical change in organizational structure to deal more effectively with issues management is not yet being advocated, but some rearrangement of managerial responsibilities may be necessary to deal with major long-term issues. Temporary issue teams are bridging departments.

Issues managers may be performing a catalyst function. The act of gathering information and analyzing it begins to draw others in, making them aware of the issue and involving them in its management.

A more deliberate discussion of business opportunities arising from issues management may be helpful because of the tendency of practitioners to focus only on the potential threats posed by issues. The success of issues management may well relate to the function's two abilities, to prevent senior management being blindsided by unexpected issues and to uncover potential opportunities upon which the corporation or organization can capitalize.

The priorities for research reflect participants' frequently expressed concern about the nature and stage of an issue's lifecycle. How to anticipate an issue before it emerges is recognized as a difficult art.

Emerging issues could be classified from within an organization as those the decision-makers are not yet aware of. Research is needed on what the term "emerging" means and how it influences the theory and practice of issues management. The term is loosely used and has at least three possible meanings, for example:

- An issue not yet well defined, or one which will emerge in some form.

- A well defined, mature issue that has yet to have an impact on the organization considering it.

- A faint signal that may or may not develop into an important issue for the organization.

A set of definitions of an emerging issue depending on circumstances and the available knowledge base may be useful. A procedure for determining whether an emerging issue will become more important could be developed. Some elements of this analysis might include:

- Does the issue affect some basic fear of the public?

- Are there large uncertainties in our information about the issue?

- Is there a link with other issues, so that this issue could emerge into prominence on the back of another issue?

Futures research may be able to contribute approaches to the early warning questions. It was suggested that issues management borrow from several disciplines in researching some of its uncertainties. For example, marketing techniques may be applied to the pretesting of strategies.

The influence of information technologies on the development of issues management and issues management research ought to be considered for their exciting potential. Massive amounts of information can be quickly retrieved, sorted, manipulated, and stored. Artificial intelligence is available to build expert systems that can help derive relationships and trends from stored information. Online databases and computers for instance can be used to:

- Develop historic data on issues as reported in the popular media,

- Test for lead-lag relationships based on an analysis of key words,

- Examine a time series of the results of annual polls against exposure given the issue in the media,

- Examine the development of issue coverage within selected media.

Table 5-1

TOPICS FOR ISSUES MANAGEMENT RESEARCH
(DEVELOPED FROM THE WORKSHOPS)

1. Early warning signals—what and where are the origins of an issue? What is the underlying trend?

2. Methods and techniques of issues management, especially the most effective and economic means of environmental scanning and screening.

3. How do you measure or evaluate success? What are the criteria? Does a formal, intentional, issues management program make a difference? What can be learned from case studies? What can cost-benefit analysis tell us?

4. The role of outside perspectives in issues management, for example, those of stockholders, customers, experts, and government.

5. Modeling issues management—concepts, implementation, validation, testing, evaluation,

   —predictive models

   —computers and expert systems

6. Pretesting and evaluation of strategies for action and intervention using tools from other fields, marketing, for example.

7. How close to corporate leadership does issues management stand? Can decision-makers learn to take risks in issues management and survive?

   —The extent of corporate awareness and use of issues management.

   —To what extent is issues management likely to change managerial practice?

Table 5-1

TOPICS FOR ISSUES MANAGEMENT RESEARCH
Continued

—The relationship of crisis management and issues management.

—Corporate social responsibility in issues management.

—The definition of an issue in organizational terms.

 8. The typology of issues, issue lifecycles.

 9. How could our concept of accounting, of measurement and reward be altered to include a perspective of future value and long-term contribution?

10. How to get the unthinkable on the table.

11. Internal issue development techniques.

12. Values and conflicts in issues management.

13. What is the optimum organizational structure for issues management?

    —Where does the issues manager fit?

    —How does issues management relate to futures research, strategic planning, and so on?

14. A survey of the field, including,

    —the most helpful types of data gathering approaches;

    —statistical methods;

    —staleness, or freshness of techniques;

    —not used, or poorly applied techniques;

Table 5-1

TOPICS FOR ISSUES MANAGEMENT RESEARCH
Continued

—a review of the management and organizational behavior
literature for material useful to issues management;

—a census of issues management programs.

15. Use of specific methods, case study development, for example,
or scenarios, in the issues management process.

16. The role of media in issues management.

17. How generic can an issues management model be?

18. Issues prioritizing and emphasis.

—weak signals;

—trigger events;

—formats;

The following items were suggested, but received only one, or no,
votes.

• What role does communications have in issues management?

• Quantitative definitions of issues.

• What are the prerequisites for acceptance of issues management
in the public and private sectors?

• Need for a theoretical framework.

• Should issues management be taught in business schools?

• The role of intuition in issues management.

Table 5-1

TOPICS FOR ISSUES MANAGEMENT RESEARCH
Continued

- Reliability of impact analysis.

- Study of international issues management techniques.

- How and when do you involve issue adversaries?

- If issues management shares a theoretical base with standard business management, what are the implications for the issues manager?

- How committees function in issues management.

Table 5-2

RESEARCHABLE TOPICS IN ISSUES MANAGEMENT

(The following list was developed from 90 telephone interviews with workshop invitees, conducted by Joseph F. Coates.)

1. Far and away, the most frequently cited topic (7 times) is where to locate issues management in the organization.

2. For many topics noted below but also as a free-standing recommendation, several people pushed for more case studies as the surest and most credible way to acquire knowledge and build understanding.

3. A most frequently raised issue was "How do you sell issues management to top managers?" As a counterpoint to this, several people cited that this is a generic and perennial issue in virtually every area.

   • How do you get "them" to pay attention to Billy Mitchell? This is a cute way of expressing the general question of how do you get management's attention? How do you promote open communication? How do you make bad news acceptable and even welcome?

   • How can you anticipate and understand management perspectives?

   • How does issues management relate to the mentality of different managers?

   • How does issues management relate to the power structure within the organization?

4. How does the structure of the firm relate to successful issues management?

5. The definition of issues management.

6. The definition of an issue.

Table 5-2

RESEARCHABLE TOPICS IN ISSUES MANAGEMENT
Continued

7. What is the proper statement of an issue in specific organizational context?

8. The sociology and the psychology of emerging issues.

9. A model is needed for how issues emerge and get public attention. Incidental to that, one should pay attention to the extent to which the system is self-fulfilling.

   - Where do issues first arise?

   - How does an issue evolve?

   - Is there a single or are there multiple models?

10. The dynamics within the company of successful and unsuccessful issues management.

11. Integrating issues management with company policies and planning.

12. How do you sensitize management to the process of issues management?

13. How do you get the treatment of issues to be pre-crisis? How do you overcome a crisis attitude?

14. How do you quantify issues?

15. How do you quantify the payoff in the management of issues?

16. Can we be more cautious and parsimonious in the use of jargon?

17. What is a successful outcome of an issue?

Table 5-2

RESEARCHABLE TOPICS IN ISSUES MANAGEMENT
Continued

18. What is a successful intervention?

   • Can you evaluate whether issues management makes a difference?

   • How do you find action options?

   • What is effective intervention action, and planning?

   • What effects have corporate actions actually had on public policy?

19. What methods and processes are characteristic of issues management? Several people cited the need for a look at technique, a review of technique, an estimate and evaluation of the quality of techniques.

   • Is there a role for electronic networks in issues management?

   • Can you improve informed judgment?

   • In workshopping, are facilitated or non-facilitated sessions best?

   • Are audio-visuals useful?

   • How do you convert data into information and then into useful action?

   • What is the role of experts?

   • Are there indicator jurisdictions?

   • Is there a role for decisions support systems?

Table 5-2

RESEARCHABLE TOPICS IN ISSUES MANAGEMENT
Continued

20. Criteria for choosing interesting futures.

21. Sensing issues earlier.

   • How do you identify issues and set priorities for dealing with them?

22. Recognize that managers and other people of the corporation are woefully ignorant of the political process; therefore, begin to educate managers along that line.

23. How do you predict outcomes?

24. How can you test strategies before their implementation?

25. How do you get an organization to adopt or adapt a process that basically does not fit its structure, organization, or outlook?

26. What programs work? (Collect specific cases.)

27. How do you deal with interest groups?

28. How do you identify stakeholders early?

29. Can one develop a super model and a common language?

30. How to make a process more systematic and less *ad hoc*.

31. Are there tip points in public opinion?

32. Work up specific case examples from the electric utility industry and then put on a road show.

33. What is the best categorization of issues?

Table 5-2

RESEARCHABLE TOPICS IN ISSUES MANAGEMENT
Continued

- Time alone is too weak a categorization.

- Are there alternative taxonomies of issues?

34. Is issues management really subsidiary to political science?

35. How do you make significantly different points of view available and disseminate them throughout the organization?

36. How do you stretch mental horizons and make the organization proactive?

37. When is it best to talk the language of the top manager, that is, the language of numbers and dollars?

38. What is the best time horizon, the best timeframe?

39. How do you get information to managers, to the lower level managers as well as the upper level?

40. Staffing of an issues management program tends to be soft. There is a dearth of economists. What is the ideal staffing?

41. Is issues management a profession?

42. How successful and important is the role of networks and coalitions?

43. Relationship of issues management to other processes, public affairs, strategic planning, etc.

44. What kinds of organizations other than the corporation can use I.M.?

45. Define an I.M. structure and process.

46. How can we legitimate teaching it in colleges and universities?

Table 5-2

RESEARCHABLE TOPICS IN ISSUES MANAGEMENT
Continued

47. Who are the issues managers and where do they come from?

48. How do you set a value on information?

49. How do you get effective feedback on actions taken?

50. Why are senior managers so resistant to the future?

51. How do we overcome the neglect of experience and lessons from other industries?

52. How do you integrate or use general trend information in identifying emerging issues?

APPENDIX A
FURTHER
ACKNOWLEDGEMENTS

Numerous people have contributed to Chapters 2-4. Among the most important of them are those who gave us the time for face-to-face or telephone interviews. The latter usually ran 30-60 minutes.

It should further be noted that many of those who were interviewed join with an even larger number of issues managers and other specialists whom we have drawn upon through their publications, public addresses, tutorials, or other materials.

The interviewees were the following:

ELECTRIC POWER RESEARCH INSTITUTE

- Stephen Baruch, Ph.D., Technical Advisor.
- Robert Catlin, Program Manager.
- Sherman Feher, Planning Analyst.
- Michael Miller, Technical Manager.
- Ralph Perhac, Ph.D., Department Director, Environmental Assessment.
- Lewis Rubin, Project Manager.
- Leonard Sagan, M.D., Senior Scientific Advisor.
- Monta Zengerle, Technical Specialist.
- Richard Zeren, Ph.D., Director, Planning and Evaluation.

EDISON ELECTRIC INSTITUTE

- Gerald Edgley, Environmental Scientist.
- Sue Lerner, Director of Corporate Planning.

ISSUES MANAGERS

- William Ashley, United Airlines, previously with Sears and McDonalds.

- Thomas M. Boller, Georgia Power Company.
- Mary Bosch, Georgia Power Company.
- Bob Dupree, Dow Chemical Company.
- Raymond P. Ewing, Allstate Insurance.
- Hank E. Koehn, Security Pacific National Bank.
- James Kostecky, Bethlehem Steel Corporation.
- Bernard Krimm, The Quaker Oats Company.
- Margaret Lehning, Internorth, Inc.
- Jack E. Nettles, Aluminum Company of America.
- David Rossiter, CONOCO.
- Jack Rushing, Allied Corporation.
- John Snow, Sears, Roebuck and Company.
- Margaret Stroup, Monsanto Corporation.

OTHERS

- Richard H. Baxter, The Roper Organization.
- Douglas Bergner, Public Affairs Council.
- W. Howard Chase, Corporate Public Issues.
- Walter Hahn, The George Washington University.
- Sean W. Kennedy, American Bankers Association.
- Dennis Little, U.S. Merit Systems Protection Board, previously with the Congressional Research Service.
- Lena Lupica, Congressional Clearinghouse on the Future.
- John F. Mancini, The Foundation for Public Affairs.
- John E. Merriam, Conference on Issues & Media.
- Martin Miller, State and Federal Associates.
- Graham T.T. Molitor, Public Policy Forecasting, Inc.
- Burt Nanus, Center for Futures Research, University of Southern California.
- William Neufeld, formerly Director of the Trend Analysis Program of the American Council of Life Insurance.
- Norman Nisenoff, Independent Consultant.
- Stephen Nowlan, Human Resources Network.
- Lewis J. Perelman, Strategic Performance Services.
- William L. Renfro, Policy Analysis Company, Inc.
- Gordon Strickland, Chemical Manufacturers Association.

Some interviewees chose not to be acknowledged.

The material in Chapter 5 is drawn from a report prepared by J.F. Coates, Inc. for EPRI, entitled *Issues Identification and Management: Developing a Research Agenda*. That report in turn was based upon a workshop in Washington, D.C., and another in Palo Alto, California; interviews conducted before the workshops; and reviews and comments on a draft of a report. We acknowledge these numerous contributors to our knowledge and to this report.

PARTICIPANTS, WASHINGTON   July 31 - August 1, 1985

Name and Organization

William G. Ashley, United Airlines
John Bagby, Penn State University
Walter G. Barlow, Research Strategies Corporation
Richard Baxter, The Roper Organization, Inc.
Hal Becker, The Futures Group, Inc.
John Brust, ALCOA
Joe Coates, J.F. Coates, Inc.
Bill Coleman, Electric Power Research Institute
Lauren Cook, Council of State Planning Agencies
Jerry Edgley, Edison Electric Institute
Lowell Endahl, National Rural Electric Cooperatives Association
Tom Fair, Department of Interior/Florida Power & Light Co.
Theron Farmer, Potomac Electric Power Co.
Sherman Feher, Electric Power Research Institute
Walter Hahn, The George Washington University
Jeff Hallett, Trend Response and Analysis Co.
Madelyn Hochstein, Yankelovich, Skelly & White
Lauri Isaacson, Northern States Power Co.
Jennifer Jarratt, J.F. Coates, Inc.
Ed Kaish, Niagara Mohawk Power Corp.
Larry Kagan, Yankelovich, Skelly & White
Kay Lee, Southern Company Services
Sue Lerner, Edison Electric Institute
Larry Logan, Edison Electric Institute
Lynn Maddox, The U.S. Department of Labor
Lynn C. Maxwell, The Tennessee Valley Authority
John Merriam, Conference on Issues and Media
Jim Morrell, Niagara Mohawk Power Corp.
Bill Neufeld, Consultant
Lewis Perelman, Strategic Performance Services
William Renfro, Policy Analysis Co., Inc./Co-Founder-Director Issues
    Management Association
Channing Riggs, Pagan International

Ralph Sullivan, The U.S. Environmental Protection Agency
Steve Wartick, Pennsylvania State University
Jane Work, National Association of Manufacturers
Frank S. Young, Electric Power Research Institute

PARTICIPANTS, PALO ALTO   August 27-28, 1985

Name and Organization

Roy Amara, Institute for the Future
Buzz Barrow, Florida Power & Light Co.
John Cassidy, California State University, San Jose
Susanne Coffey, Pacific Gas & Electric Co.
Ashton B. Collins, Jr., RCI Consulting Group
Jay Creutz, Management Analysis Co.
Jerry Edgley, Edison Electric Institute
Sherman Feher, Electric Power Research Institute
Paul S. Feldman, Pennsylvania Electric Co.
Shel Feldman, Opinion Research Corporation
Victor Furtado, Pacific Gas & Electric Co.
Dominic Geraghty, Electric Power Research Institute
J. Phillip Halstead, Clorox Co.
Spencer Hathaway, The Hathaway Group
Michael M. Hertel, Southern California Edison Co.
Kenneth W. Hunter, U.S. General Accounting Office
Jennifer Jarratt, J.F. Coates, Inc.
Jean Logsdon, University of Santa Clara, School of Management
Austin Marx, Hewlett Packard Corp.
Bernard McNair, Southern California Edison Co.
Carol Meyers, Arizona Public Service Co.
Katherine A. Miller, Electric Power Research Institute
Bill Neufeld, Consultant
Randall Scheel, Consultant
Henry A. Tombari, California State University, Hayward, School of Business
    & Economics
Marilyn Wright, Georgia Power Co.
Oliver Yu, Electric Power Research Institute
Richard W. Zeren, Electric Power Research Institute

CONTRIBUTORS

    Most of those who participated in the workshops were interviewed before
the meetings. Those who were interviewed and were not able to attend either

session are included here. This list also includes those who reviewed and commented on a draft of this report.

Name and Organization

Michael Annison, The Westrend Group, Ltd.
H. Igor Ansoff, U.S. International University
Linda Curry Bartholomew, Pennsylvania Power and Light Co.
Mike Bergman, American Public Power Association
Douglas Bergner, Public Affairs Council
Ross Bishop, Consultant
Mary Bosch, Georgia Power Co.
Wayne Boucher, Hotchkiss, Born & Boucher
Arnold Brown, Weiner, Edrich, Brown
Rogene Buchholz, University of Texas at Dallas
Richard Butrick, County Supervisors Assn. of Calif.
W. Howard Chase, Howard Chase Enterprises, Inc.
Phillip Cochran, Penn State University
Craig Conley, Southern California Edison
Michael Cutler, GTE Sprint Communications
Roger Davis, Salt River Project
Herb Dreyer, Strategic Moves
Raymond P. Ewing, Allstate Insurance Co.
Andrew Gollner, Concordia University
Barbara Gray, Penn State University
Jack Hamilton, E. I. Du Pont de Nemours and Co., Inc.
Chuck Harvel, Public Service Co. of New Mexico
Jon C. Holtzman, Chemical Manufacturers Association
Jim Hulden, Portland General Electric Co.
Elliot Kline, University of the Pacific
Hank Koehn, Trimtab Consulting Group
James F. Kostecky, Bethlehem Steel Corp.
Louis G. Laughlin, Security Pacific National Bank
Dennis Little, The Merit Systems Protection Board
Lena Lupica, Early Signals
Kathleen MacDonough, General Foods Corp.
George Marotta, Hoover Institution
Joseph P. Martino, University of Dayton
Jay S. Mendell, Florida Atlantic University
Martin Miller, State & Federal Associates
Graham T. T. Molitor, Public Policy Forecasting, Inc.
Donald Piepenburg, Wisconsin Power and Light Co.
John Reuss, The U.S. Environmental Protection Agency

W. David Rossiter, CONOCO, Inc.
Lewis Rubin, Electric Power Research Institute
Robert Rude, New York State Electric & Gas Co.
David Rusk, Public Service Co. of New Mexico
Richard Sawaya, Atlantic Richfield Co.
Jackie Siminitus, Human Resources Network
James B. Smith, SRI International
Peter Strauss, Consultant
Carl Tripp, Union Carbide
Bertram Wakeley, Office of the Governor, State of New Hampshire
Ian Wilson, SRI International
Roger Yott, Portland General Electric Co.
R.D. Zentner, University of Houston Law School

BIBLIOGRAPHY

Armstrong, J.S. *Long-Range Forecasting*. New York: John Wiley & Sons, 1978.

Ascher, W. *Forecasting: An Appraisal for Policy Makers and Planners*. Baltimore: The Johns Hopkins University Press, 1978.

Ascher, W., and Overholt, W.H. *Strategic Planning and Forecasting: Political Risk and Economic Opportunity*. New York: John Wiley & Sons, 1983.

Ayres, R.V. *Technological Forecasting and Long-Range Planning*. New York: McGraw-Hill, 1969.

Bell System Emerging Issues Program. Basking Ridge, NJ: A.T.&T. Co., April 1980.

Brown, J.K. *This Business of Issues: Coping with the Company's Environments*. New York: The Conference Board, 1979.

Campbell, T.W. "Identifying the Issues." *Public Relations Journal* 39 (August 1983), 19-20.

Chase, W. Howard, ed. *Corporate Public Issues*. Stamford, CT: IAP, April 1976.

———. *Issues Management: Origins of the Future*. Stamford, CT: IAP, 1984.

Coates, Joseph F. "Foresight in Federal Government Policymaking." *Futures Research Quarterly* (Summer 1985), 29-53.

———. "The Role of Formal Models in Technology Assessment." *Technological Forecasting and Social Change* 9 (Spring 1976), 139-190.

———. "A Technology Assessment Tool Kit." *Chem Tech* (June 1976), 372-383. Reprinted in *Handbook of Futures Research*, edited by Jib Fowles, Westport, CT: Greenwood Press, 1978, 397-421.

———. "What is a Public Policy Issue?" *Interdisciplinary Science Reviews* 4:1 (1979), 27-44.

———. "Why Think About the Future: Some Administrative-Political Perspectives." *Public Administration Review* 5 (September/October 1976), 580-585.

Connor, F.J. "Issues Management at American Can Company." Reprinted by American Can Company from a speech given at the Issues Management Association Fall Conference, November 1983.

Enzer, S. "INTERAX - An Interactive Model for Studying Future Business Environments: Parts I and II." *Technological Forecasting and Social Change* XVII (1980), 141-159, 211-242.

Ewing, R.P. "Evaluating Issues Management." *Public Relations Journal* 36 (June 1980), 14-16.

———. "The Use of Futurist Techniques in Issues Management." *Public Relations Quarterly* 22:8 (Winter 1979), 15-19.

Fowles, J., ed. *Handbook of Futures Research*. Westport, CT: Greenwood Press, 1978. From *Part III*, "The Procedures of Futures Research":

    I.H. Wilson. "Scenarios." 225-247.

    K.Q. Hill. "Trend Extrapolation." 249-272.

    H.A. Linstone. "The Delphi Technique." 273-300.

    J.G. Stover and T.J. Gordon. "Cross-Impact Analysis." 301-328.

    J.M. McLean. "Simulation Modeling." 329-352.

    R.D. Duke. "Simulation Gaming." 353-367.

Garvin, C.C., Jr. "The Future Has a Mind of Its Own." *The Lamp* 66:1 (Spring 1984), 1-2.

Godiwalla, Y. "Environmental Scanning—Does it Help the Chief Executive?" *Long Range Planning* 13:5 (October 1980), 87-99.

Gollner, A.B. *Social Change and Corporate Strategy*. Stamford, CT: IAP, 1984.

Halal, W.E. "Strategic Management: The State-of-the-Art and Beyond." *Technological Forecasting and Social Change* 25 (1984), 239-261.

Hamilton, J.H. "Issues Management." (Presentation to a meeting of the Issues Management Association, Washington, D.C., June 1984.)

Hegarty, W.H. "Strategic Planning in the 1980's—Coping with Complex External Forces." *Planning Review* 40 (1981), 8-12, 40.

Helmer, O. *Looking Forward: A Guide to Futures Research*. Beverly Hills, CA: Sage Publications, 1983.

Holsti, Ole R. *Content Analysis for the Social Sciences and Humanities*. Reading, MA: Wesley Publishing Company, 1969.

"Issues Management: The Corporation Gets Tough." *AMA Management Review* 71:5 (May 1982), 4.

Jain, Subhash, C. "Environmental Scanning in U.S. Corporations." *Long Range Planning* 17 (April 1984), 117-128.

Jones, B.L., and Chase, W.H. "Issue Management." *Public Relations Review* 5 (Summer 1979), 2.

Kallman, E.A., and Reinharth, L. *Information Systems for Planning and Decision Making*. New York: Van Nostrand Reinhold, 1984.

Kahn, Herman, and Wiener, Anthony. *The Year 2000: A Framework for Speculation on the Next Thirty-Three Years*. New York: MacMillan, 1967.

Kane, J. "A Primer for a New Cross-Impact Language—KSIM." *Technological Forecasting and Social Change* 4 (1972), 129-142.

Klein, H.E., and Linneman, R. "The Use of Scenarios in Corporate Planning—Eight Case Histories." *Long Range Planning* 14:5 (October, 1981), 49-77.

Klein, H.E., and Newman, W.H. "How to Integrate New Environmental Forces into Strategic Planning." *Management Review* 69:7 (July 1980), 40-48.

Lindenmann, W.K. "Content Analysis." *Public Relations Journal* 39:7 (July 1983), 24.

Linneman, R.E., and Klein, H.E. "The Use of Multiple Scenarios by U.S. Industrial Companies." *Long Range Planning* 12 (1979), 83-90.

Linstone, H.A., and Turoff, M., eds. *The Delphi Method: Techniques and Application*. Reading, MA: Addison-Wesley, 1975.

Long Range Planning. Special Issue on Forecasting 15:4 (August 1982):
  Beck, P.W. "Corporate Planning for an Uncertain Future." 3.
  King, W.R. "Using Strategic Issue Analysis." 5.
  Holloway, C., and J.A. Pearce II. "Computer Assisted Strategic Planning." 6.
  Preble, J.F. "Futures Forecasting with LEAP." 6-7.
  Jonsson, S., and I. Petzall. "Forecasting Political Decisions and Their Impact on Business." 9-10.
  Nanus, B. "QUEST—Quick Environmental Scanning Technique." 12-13.

McCosh, A.M., Rahman, M., and Earl, M.J. *Developing Managerial Information Systems*. London: Macmillan, 1982.

MacNulty, C.A.R. "Scenario Development for Corporate Planning." *Futures* 9:2 (1977), 128-138.

Martino, J.P. *Technological Forecasting for Decision Making*. 2d ed. New York-North Holland: Elsevier Scientific Publishing Co., 1983.

Molitor, G.T.T. "Plotting the Patterns of Change." *Enterprise* (March 1984), 4-9.

Morrison, J.L., Renfro, W.L., and Boucher, W.I., eds. *Applying Methods and Techniques of Futures Research*. San Francisco: Jossey-Bass, Inc., 1982:
  Renfro, W.L., and J.L. Morrison. Chapter 1, "The Scanning Process: Getting Started." 5-20. Chapter 2, "The Scanning Process: Methods and Uses." 21-37.
  Heydinger, R.B., and R.D. Zentner. Chapter 4, "Multiple Scenario Analysis: Introducing Uncertainty into the Planning Process." 51-68.
  Enzer, S. Chapter 5, "New Directions in Futures Methodology." 69-83.

Nagelschmidt, J.S., ed. *The Public Affairs Handbook*. Washington, D.C.: Fraser/Associates and AMACOM, Div. of American Management Associations, 1982:
  Part Three: "Public Policy."

      Hart, A.S. "Identifying Issues." 74-80.

      Tortorello, N.J. "Uses of Polling." 85-91.

      Zentner, R. "Survey Research." 92-104.

      Chase, W.H. "Issues Management." 104-109.

    Part Four: "Government Relations."

      Renfro, W. "Forecasting Issues." 134-143.

      Martin, J.L. "Public Affairs: The State View." 143-147.

      Martin, F.J., Jr. "Public Affairs: The Corporate/State View." 148-153.

      Grefe, E.A. "Political Education." 154-163.

Nowlan, S.E., and Shayon, D.R., eds. *Leveraging the Impact of Public Affairs: A Guidebook Based on Practical Experience for Corporate Public Affairs Executives.* Philadelphia: Human Resources Network, 1984.

Nanus, B. "The Corporate Futurist." *The World Future Society Bulletin* XV (March-April 1981), 12-14.

Pearce, J.A., II, Chapman, B.L., and David, F.R. "Environmental Scanning for Small and Growing Firms." *Journal of Small Business Management* (July 1982), 27-34.

Perham, J. "New Company Watchdog." *Dun's Business Month* 118:6 (December 1981), 88-89.

Porter, A.L. *A Guidebook for Technology Assessment and Impact Analysis.* New York: Elsevier Science Publishing Co., 1980.

Preble, J.F. "Corporate Use of Environmental Scanning." *University of Michigan Business Review* (September 1978), 121-127.

———. "Public Sector Use of the Delphi Technique." *Technological Forecasting and Social Change* 23 (1983), 75-88.

Quade, E.S. *Analysis for Public Decisions.* 2d ed. New York: Elsevier Science Publishing Co., 1982.

Renfro, W.L. (ed.) *CongressScan: The Legislative Regulatory Service.* Washington, D.C.: Policy Analysis Company, Inc. Monthly.

———. *The Legislative Role of Corporations.* Special Study #79. New York: American Management Association, 1983.

———. "Managing the Issues of the 1980's." *The Futurist* XVI (August 1982), 61-66.

——— and J.L. Morrison. "Merging Two Futures Concepts: Issues Management and Policy Impact Analysis." *The Futurist* XV (October 1982), 54-56.

———. "Policy Impact Analysis: A Step Beyond Forecasting." *World Future Society Bulletin* 14:4 (July/August 1980), 19-26.

Riggs, Walter E. "The Delphi Technique: An Experimental Evaluation." *Technological Forecasting and Social Change* 23 (1983), 89-94.

Rucks, A.C., and Ginter, P.M. "Strategic Models and Simulations: An Emerging Decision-Making Aid." *Journal of Systems Management* (June 1984), 12-16.

Sekiguchi, H.S., and Storey, S.I. "Strategic Planning Practices of Investor-Owned Electric Utilities." *Managerial Planning* (May/June 1983), 45-51.

Sprague, R.H. "A Framework for the Development of Decision Support Systems." In Kallman, E.A., and Reinharth, L., eds., op.cit. 29-53.

Terry, P.T. "Mechanisms for Environmental Scanning." *Long Range Planning* 10:3 (June 1977), 2-9.

Vanderwicken, P. "'Externalysis': A New Dimension in Planning." *Planning Review* 45 (July 1982), 24-27.

Walsh, D. "Utilities Come in From the Darkness." *American Demographics* 6:6 (June 1984), 29-31.

Weiner, E. "Future Scanning for Trade Groups and Companies." *Harvard Business Review* 54:5 (September/October 1976), 14, 174-176.

Wheelwright, S.C., and Makridakis, S. *Forecasting Methods for Management.* 2d ed. New York: Wiley Interscience Series, 1977.

Zentner, R.D. "Forecasting Emerging Issues." Presented at the Fourth General Assembly of the World Future Society. July 1982.

———. "Forecasting Public Issues." *The Futurist* 18:3 (June 1984), 25-29.

———. "Scenarios, Past, Present and Future." *Long Range Planning* 15:3 (1982), 12-20.

INDEX

American Council of Life Insurance, 33, 53, 65.
American Petroleum Institute, 61.
AT&T, 21, 64, 67.
ALCOA, 89.
Allied Chemical Company, 27, 65.
Allstate, 27.
Applied Futures, Inc., 77.
ARCO, 21.

Bell, Daniel, 4, 21.
Bellwether jurisdictions, 54, 56, 68.
Boucher, W., 114.
Brainstorming, 86.
Brainwriting, 86.
Brown, J.K., 102.

Cambridge Reports, Inc., 60.
Causal loop diagrams, 86.
Center for Futures Research (University of Southern California), 79.
Charrette, 86.
Chemical Manufacturers Association, 64.
CEO (Chief Executive Officer), role of, 25.
Coates, Joseph F., 1.
Column inch counting, 57.
Council of State Planning Agencies, 56.
Commerce Clearinghouse, 70.
Computer assisted techniques, 83-85.
Condorcet, Marquis de, 54.
Conference Board, The, 21, 97, 102.

Conference telephone calls, 86.
Conflict, issues as, 19.
Congressional Clearinghouse on the Future, 21.
Congressional Research Service, Library of Congress, 21, 69.
Congress Scan, 69.
Consensor, 77, 85.
Consequence diagrams, 86.
Content analysis, 66.
Conversational Delphi, 75-77, 85.
Corporate culture, 15, 38.
Correlation and regression, 95.
Cross impact analysis, 78-80.

Decision support systems, 80-82, 83.
Delphi, 70-75, 83, 85.
Dow Chemical Company, 61.
Dresner, Morris & Tortorello, 60.
DSS (See decision support systems)

Economic analysis, 94.
Emerging issues, 19-21.
    characteristics of, 19.
    identification of, 30.
Environmental Protection Agency, U.S., 21.
Environment of an organization, 17.
Evaluation matrices, 102.
Executive Committee, role of, 25.
Expert panels, 65.

Forecasting, definition of, 11.
Foresight, 8-13.
    definition of, 11.
Fowles, J., 90.

Futures Research, 6-7.
    relationship to issues
      management, 114.

Gaming, 86.
General Electric Co., 21, 61, 68, 87,
  89.
Ginter, P.M., 83.

Hill & Knowlton, Inc., 67.
Holloway, C., 83.

IBM, 65.
Ideawriting, 86.
INTERAX, 79-80.
Interpretive structural modeling, 86.
International Policy, 70.
Interviews, (See Conversational
  Delphi)
Issue briefs, 36.
Issues as conflicts, 19.
Issues identification, 32-37.
  and management, 17.
Issues management:
  assumptions, 18, 97.
  benefits from, 112.
  conceptual model, 29.
  conditions for success, 16.
  conditions for an effective
    program, 25.
  education in, 37.
  getting started, 98.
  limitations on, 43.
  location in the organization,
    98, 104.
  organizing for, 32-44.
  system, 98-105.
  techniques, 52-95.
  team, 99.
Issues Management Association, 52,
  97.
Issues Management Letter, 57.
Issues manager, 99.

Issues modeling, 95.

J.F. Coates, Inc., 29, 46, 88.
Jones, Reginald H., 21.
Jury of executive opinion, 62.

Kahn, Herman, 87.
Kane, J., 78.
Key player analysis, 94.
KISS principle, 27.
KSIM, 78, 80, 86.

Lawless, Edward W., 23.
Legislate, 70.
Legislative tracking, 68.
LegiScan, 69, 70.
Lenz, Ralph, 34, 35.
Life Cycle, (See Public Policy Issue)
Lindenmann, W.K., 67.
Louis Harris & Associates, 60, 65.

Media analysis, 57, 68.
Methods and techniques, 45-92
    Evaluation factors, 48-52.
Mock processes, 86.
Model, definition of, 11.
Molitor, G., 23, 24, 54.
Monitoring issues, 30.
Monitoring report format, 35.
Monsanto Corporation, 21, 61, 63,
  79.
Monte Carlo technique, 84.

Naisbitt Group, 55, 67, 68.
Nagelschmidt, J.S., 61.
National Association of Manu-
  facturers, 21, 22, 27, 64, 97.
National Agricultural Chemical
  Association, 61.
National Center for Legislative
  Research, 70.
News Analysis Institute, 67.
Networking, 41, 52, 101.

Nominal group technique, 86.

Occurrence matrix, 102.
OTA, (Office of Technology Assessment, U.S. Congress), 21.
Opinion Research Corporation, 60.

Panels, (See Expert Panels).
Pearce, J.A., 83.
Picturephone conference, 86.
Pitney Bowes, 21.
PPG Industries, 21.
Planning Executives Institute, 83.
Policy Analysis Company, 69.
Policy capturing, 86.
Polls, 59.
Post-industrial society, 4.
PR Data Systems, 67.
Precursor analysis, 54, 56, 68.
Priorities, 110.
Public Affairs Council, 53, 64.
Public Affairs Inflow, 70.
Public Opinion, 59.
Public Opinion Quarterly, 60.
Public Policy Forecasting, Inc., 24.
Public policy issues, 19-24.
    lifecycle of, 21.
    model, 22.
Public Service Company of Colorado, 61.

QSIM, 86.

Rand Corporation, 71.
Research:
    agenda in issues management, 116-125.
    needs in issues management, 108-109.
    priorities in issues management, 110-111.
    role in issues management, 108-9.

Risks, 5.
Role playing, 86.
Roper Organization, The, 60.
Rucks, A.C., 83.

Scanning, 30, 100.
Scanning report format, 34.
Scenarios, 87-95.
Schneider, Hans-Jochen, 82.
Sears Roebuck & Co., 21.
Sensitivity analysis, 95.
Sentry Insurance Company, 61.
Shell Oil Company, 27, 61.
Signed digraphs, 86.
Small group processes, 85-86.
Sperry Rand, 21.
Sprague, Ralph, 81.
State and Federal Associates, 56.
State Policy, 56.
STEP, 52.
Strategic planning, 30.
Surveys, 59.

TAP, 33, 53, 65.
Technology and Social Shock, 23.
Telephone conference, 86.
The Year 2000: A Framework for Speculation on the Next Thirty-Three Years, 87.
This Business of Issues: Coping with the Company's Environment, 102.
Trend Report, 68.
Trendex, 61.
Trends:
    long-term, 2-4.
    extrapolation, 94.
Trigger events, 94.
TRW, 71.

United Airlines, 21, 27.
U.S. General Accounting Office, 21.
United Way, 21, 52.

Van Deerlin, Lionel, 70.

Warfield, John N., 87.
Weiner Edrich Brown, Inc., 52, 65.
Westinghouse, 34, 35.
Whinston, A., 82.
Wiener, A., 87.
Wilson, Ian, 87.

Work, Jane, 21-22.

Xerox, 65.

Yankelovich, Skelly and White, Inc., 60.

Zentner, R.D., 61.